HOW TO BE A
BANDLEADER

Not just the man of the hour—but the bandleader of a generation!
Man of many comebacks and no retirements, Paul Whiteman will
still be a contender when today's stars have flickered out.

HOW TO BE A
BANDLEADER

By PAUL WHITEMAN
and
LESLIE LIEBER

WILDSIDE PRESS

CONTENTS

ILLUSTRATIONS

7

8   Illustrations

HOW TO BE A
BANDLEADER

FOREWORD

TIME has wrought a change in a very important term used in this book—the word "bandleader." A few years ago, "bandleader" meant the man who led a military march down Main Street or staged a band concert every Sunday in the park. The word "band" was used only in speaking of instruments adapted for playing on the march. For outdoor use these had to be both loud and portable, thus eliminating the piano and all the stringed instruments. Bands, therefore, became synonymous with "brass." If you led a combination which boasted both brass and strings, you were then an orchestra conductor. Today, however, "band" is used loosely to signify any combination of instruments assembled for the performance of music. The modern dance orchestra or band usually consists of four saxophones, three trumpets, three trombones, a piano, guitar, drums and bass violin. Society orchestras often subtract brass and add strings, but a mixture of military and "civilian" instruments is necessary in some form.

Before the first World War, "bandleader" meant Patrick Gilmore or John Philip Sousa, "The March King." These played thrilling music and attracted large audiences on annual tours of the nation's concert stages. But in some localities years would elapse between reappearances of these monster organizations. To take up the slack, nearly every village in the country produced its own Sunday concerts. Each band played just like the one upstate, downstate, or in the next state. Reading identical arrangements of "Stars and Stripes Forever," they strove for uniformity and not individuality.

Orchestras hired to furnish dance music also did a business-like job. In Cincinnati, "After the Ball" sounded exactly the way it did in New York where fifty other orchestras gave it the approved rubber-stamp treatment. There were never any entranced souls willing to stand around for the pure joy of listening, and there was no reason to import out-of-town orchestras noted for "different styles." In 1900, with only seven symphony orchestras in the whole country, leading a band often meant joining the marines. Sousa's fame resulted from his success with the United States Marine Band, which he modeled after the world-renowned *Garde Républicaine* in France. No mass ambition to be a bandleader could logically exist in those days. For it took only a handful of conductors to fill the nation's quota.

Suddenly, around 1917, the germ of the modern dance band came into being. A small five-piece combination of jazz experts, called the Original Dixieland Jazz Band, breezed up from New Orleans and took New York by storm. They opened on January 26, 1917, at Riesenweber's famous restaurant on Columbus Circle. Their specialty was frenzied jazz, collectively improvised, and brimming over with a kind of rhythmical abandon never heard before in the big city. When the opening night guests at Riesenweber's heard this newfangled jazz, they were too nonplussed to move. They just stood and gaped. It was the first time a New York audience had looked twice at a dance musician. It wasn't the last.

Another group of jazz evangelists, starting out about the same time from New Orleans ended up in Chicago. Among them were "King" Oliver, Johnny Dodds, Sidney Bechet, Zutty Singleton, and Louis Armstrong, originally trumpeter with Fate Marable's orchestra on the *Dixie Belle*, a Mississippi River excursion steamboat.

To the spreading influence of pure New Orleans and Memphis jazz, came two civilizing notes from California. Art Hickman, orchestrating some of the rawness out of the new product, came east and took his big band into Ziegfeld's Midnight Frolic. He was the first leader to develop teamwork by several saxophones, featuring brilliant runs and counterpoint by Clyde Doerr, one of the finest virtuosos of the period. Doerr wasn't a hot man, but his melodic intertwinings were tasteful and helped keep alive the inventive spirit of the new music.

Whatever ripple Hickman had created in New York night-club and theatre circles was as nothing compared to the sensational success of another import from California, Paul Whiteman. The fullhouse ropes went up an hour after Lord and Lady Mountbatten and other celebrities had taken their tables at the old Palais Royal. Since then the ropes have always been up for Whiteman—enough rope to hang a lot of the competition. Whiteman's nine men played special arrangements made by Ferdie Grofé, the band's piano player and one of the finest orchestrators America has produced.

Around this time Whiteman made records like "Whispering" and "Song of India," which sold millions of copies. In February, 1924, Paul Whiteman surprised the musical world by taking his augmented orchestra in to Aeolian Hall for the first high-brow jazz concert in history. Victor Herbert contributed an original suite of music for the occasion and

George Gershwin's "Rhapsody in Blue" received its premiere performance. After a three-hour program which included "Barn Yard Blues," and "Yes, We Have No Bananas," the audience of blue-ribbon musicians and classical critics went home with a new idea of the brilliant possibilities inherent in a modern orchestra.

From then on, jazz, the precursor of swing, was proclaimed respectable. It was fit to eat by—and if there was still the objection of loudness, Whiteman also removed that. According to music-critic Deems Taylor, who happened to attend the 1924 Aeolian Concert, Whiteman was the first conductor to make jazz a commodity salable to hotels. "Before Paul came along," says Mr. Taylor, "jazz was too raucous to qualify as dinner music. Whiteman realized the value of understatement. In other words, he subdued his saxophones and muted his trumpets. When hotel men realized that jazz no longer interfered either with conversation or digestion, orchestra leaders found a new market for their wares."

Since then that market has grown steadily in all fields of entertainment. Undoubtedly the greatest factor in this development has been the radio. A week's broadcasting today is worth years of barnstorming around the country. Radio has increased a thousandfold the number of bandleaders known to the public. Even more important than the radio is the demand that youthful dance music be furnished by young musicians. In Europe it made no difference if the musicians were old enough to be the grandfathers of the young partners whirling away on the dance floor. Over there, the dancing, the music, and the musicians were all equally aged. But in America, the music is new. Musicians must be almost as young as those who dance to it. And a nation's orchestra leaders, for the first time, now come from the ranks of youngsters barely out of their teens.

The modern orchestra occupies a unique position in the history of music. It is not wholly a dance orchestra. As many as 21,000 people may jam the Paramount Theatre in a single day just to hear a good swing band. Next day they'll rush someplace else just to dance to it. That's why a modern orchestra must be not only a musical organization but a complete stage act in itself. It may be called upon to make a Hollywood movie, appear for long theatre engagements, or produce a half-hour radio show on a coast-to-coast hookup. America today is honeycombed with orchestras. There's plenty of room at the top, and this country can absorb a greater number of first-rate bandleaders with every passing year.

But you don't have to be one of the topnotch

leaders to make your living at music. Where there was once a village band, there's room today for three or four crackerjack dance outfits. "Territory" bands, even though they never acquire national reputations, abound and prosper in every part of the country. So don't think you have to reach the very summit to make good as a bandleader. There's only one President of the United States, but there are thousands of Mayors of Municipalities in this country. Those who can't make the grade nationally, can at least strive for top place in their own locality. In the struggle to reach the top you'll need two weapons —sharp wits and a musical instrument.

The authors wish to acknowledge with gratitude the invaluable assistance of Hal Davis, Stephanie Lieber and Phil Cohan.

L. L.

Gene Krupa, one of the finest white drummers, has a standing invitation to join Arturo Toscanini's symphony orchestra. Judging from this picture, Gene would rather lead his own swing outfit.

The resonant, romantic voice of Vaughn Monroe has done more than the Mt. Wilson Observatory to popularize the moon. Notice his southpaw technique in signing autographs.

CHAPTER I

SO YOU WANT TO LEAD
A BAND?

WITH still a minute to go before air time, the
stage of the huge radio playhouse is all set for
action. Six microphones, like motors of transport
liners before flight, are getting last-minute check-
ups from a radio engineer who test-twists dials in a
glass-enclosed booth to the right of the stage. Even
this technician in a cage wears a tuxedo, for this is
an important occasion. Right now the theatre sounds
like a boiler factory. A dozen or so jazz musicians
are blowing their favorite warming-up exercises for
all they're worth. They make a noise no music critic
has ever succeeded in describing, but it's exactly the
same din as symphony musicians create in their
preconcert tune-ups.

In a darkened glass compartment to the left
of the stage sit the program's sponsors, business-
men who pay fantastic sums of money to put this
half-hour broadcast on the air. They've invested

heavily in some young bandleader because they're sure his name has power . . . sufficient power, glamour and popularity to make listeners all over the country buy the product associated with his name on the air. A capacity crowd of thirteen hundred of these staunch admirers are squeezed into the studio right now, impatient for the official sound of the band.

A radio stage has no footlights. This makes it easy for the announcer to stand at the front of the stage and instruct the spectators to get all the coughing out of their systems within sixty seconds. All at once, attention switches again to the orchestra. A trombonist has tripped over the guitarist's music stand in a hurried scramble for his seat. Quip on the trigger, the announcer jokes about the slip of the slip-horn player. The audience laughs, but grows tense again as the announcer glances at the big second hand of the wall clock. Suddenly a spotlight picks up a figure in the wings and trails a trim young man as he moves quickly to the center of the stage. A pandemonium of applause breaks loose and subsides quickly as a red "on the air" sign flashes above the control booth. The bandleader gives an imperceptible wrist-twist which seems to turn a spigot that lets loose a flood of music. His theme song—synonymous with his name to millions of listeners—is

A tense moment in an important coast-to-coast broadcast. Horace Heidt and his Musical Knights, aided by three queens in the fiddle section, back up the large choral group.

being carried by over a hundred radio stations to every corner of America!

Perhaps all this has sounded to you like an unduly long minute. But that's how long minutes last when they precede such things as "play ball" yells, or "on the air" signals. And that's how long minutes seem when a person collects $280 for each one that passes. You see, that young orchestra leader, who isn't handsome enough to be a movie star, educated enough to be a lawyer or old enough to be a business executive, is already drawing a larger salary than most people in any of those other fields. He, too, stands at the head of a corporation—a corporation critically audited every day by untold numbers of listeners. His orchestra is a concern in which every young music fan in the country has a share. These young shareholders vote the orchestra up or down on the market. And if you want to see where it stands today, just read the listings of nation-wide polls conducted by *Down Beat* and *Metronome*, two of the outstanding jazz man's magazines. The leader makes more money per year than the President of the United States; and some of his older colleagues have lasted more than three terms—without apologizing. Those sponsors pay $8,500 to the young maestro for a half-hour of his distinctive music. And as a result of the tremendous publicity value of these nation-wide broadcasts, the leader can collect as much as $2,000 for one-night engagements during the rest of the week.

Kay Kyser, for example, playing at the Civic Auditorium in Pasadena, California, took in a one-night record figure of $9,000 in paid admissions. That's big money, no matter how you slice it. A name outfit usually gets $2,000 for each college date, and Glen Gray has played more than 400 of these university proms since the band's debut. Combine the proms with long hotel engagements, sponsored radio shows, stage appearances, recording sessions and one-night dancehall stands, and you'll get some idea of the dollar side of bandleading. Many parents like to have their sons choose a business career. Well, manufacturing dance music is more than just a business career. It's a growing $110,000,000-a-year industry which will always need men. There's reward enough at the top to justify the hard work ahead of you—if you want to be a bandleader.

The big money earned by bandleaders has helped indirectly to eliminate some of the disrespect that once surrounded the life of a musician. I mention this because everybody, naturally, wants to choose a profession that carries prestige and merits the respect of his family and friends. Once upon a time—and that was a long time ago—musicians were treated like dishwashers. They had to come in the side door and eat their refreshments in the kitchen. And that, by itself, gives some indication of the lack of esteem in which they were held by society. It's pretty hard to unearth the origin of this foolish prejudice. Maybe it began because playing an instrument was once regarded as a sort of hand labor. But more likely this disdain goes back to ancient times when the musician, half stooge and half servant, played at great events without directly participating in them. Musicians "accompanied" chariot races at the Olympic games. Romans boxed to the sound of flutes. Royalty ate while underlings strummed on a lyre. Monarchs made impressive entrances while flunkies in knee breeches blared on trumpets. When somebody important was about to die, the watchword was, "Now you can send for the flute players." In others words, everybody worthwhile raced, boxed, made a hero of himself and died—except the flute players. All they did was pucker their lips and receive non-union wages.

America has changed all that. Bandleaders have become national heroes, midnight, morning and matinee idols. The bass player in Gillespie's orchestra is as well-known to youngsters of a certain age as the first-base player with the St. Louis Browns. Of course, when it comes to entertaining visiting royalty with "American music," the White House thinks in terms of Kate Smith and John Charles Thomas. But in Europe many ruling families have listened respectfully to hot jazz. Louis Armstrong gave a command performance for the late King George, and Queen Mary. The proceedings probably won't be recorded in any memoirs of the reign, but right in the middle of a hot chorus, Louis took the trumpet from his lips and shouted, "I'se swingin' it fo' you, Rex." King Zog of Albania kept a hot jazz band on tap in his palace, and Alfonso XIII of Spain ordered several command performances of swing stars who were on tour of Europe. Of course, none of these monarchs sits on a throne today, but I don't think jazz had anything to do with that. On Duke Ellington's last visit to England, the Duke of Kent, possessor of one of the world's finest hot record collections, picked out Ellington's "Swampy River" on the piano while the visiting bandsman chatted over cocktails with the Prince of Wales. Incidentally, the Prince, now the Duke of Windsor, once played drums in Hal Kemp's orchestra, non-professionally, of course. Mussolini told the late newspaper correspondent, Webb Miller, that he listened to jazz on phonograph records. He also fiddled—probably more like Nero than Joe Venuti.

In America, swing music with its loose, free and imaginative way of playing will some day gain recognition in the highest quarters. For, no matter how you look at it, the jitterbugs of today—that is, the vast majority of young enthusiasts who love swing music—will some day grow up and run this nation. Perhaps seven of the Nine Old Men of the Supreme Court Bench will be able to interpret "Honeysuckle Rose" as well as the Constitution. A majority of Congress, voting as ex-jitterbugs, may commission a great sculptor to chisel Duke Ellington's face out of the side of a mountain. Probably that's expecting a little too much; but at any rate, you will be proud to be a musician. As a profession in America, it's on the upswing in every way.

I don't mean to give the idea that all the emphasis should be on money and respect. Those are only side issues, and shouldn't make a single convert for the bandleader business. In fact, if fame and fortune are your chief incentives, you'd do well to steer clear of a calling which places a firm, steady love of music above all else. Few of the men for whom bands are named today started out with do-or-die intentions to become a leader. They started out with an intense love of a musical instrument. Then they devoted years of their lives to mastering it. They put in an endless amount of practice, years

Jitterbugs in Congress? Not yet, but Benny Goodman seems to feel quite at home in the Senate Restaurant ad-libbing table talk with (l. to r.) the late Secretary of Labor Schwellenbach, ex-Senator LaFollette of Wisconsin, Senator Minton of Indiana and Gardner Jackson, prominent Washingtonian.

of drudgery and hard knocks in scores of bands; they suffered disappointments on jobs, spent sleepless nights on long bus hops, accepted salary cuts— but they always managed to plod ahead in the one thing that really counted—their musical instrument.

You've got to be a musician through and through to play in a topnotch band today. But you've got to be even more than a musician to be its leader. Don't ask yourself how much you love money and glory. That doesn't determine your fitness to lead a band. Ask yourself whether you care for your saxophone or your trumpet as much as a human being can care for any inanimate object. For you must have the musical power to turn that instrument into something animate! It must be made to express whatever poetry of music you have in you. Then, when you surpass the others in your field, when you command the respect of your fellow instrumentalists, you may be ready to stand up in front of them.

Having played viola in symphony orchestras and in the well-known Minetti String Quartet before the formation of my jazz orchestra on the coast, I am naturally not a novice. However, let me be frank. I did not play viola or violin like a Joe Venuti. I improvised a little too much for symphony orchestras but not quite enough for jazz. The violin's response to my touch never quite matched the love

I felt for it or for my music. In getting to the top and staying there, I arrived without too much assistance from the fiddle. But times have completely changed. I started out on the ground floor of the business! Today the field is crowded and the competition is terribly stiff. What was possible twenty years ago cannot be duplicated by a beginner today. For you, there is only one way to achieve self-distinction and that's through mastery of an instrument. That is the only open sesame to success for the bandleader of the future. Swing is a matter of interpretation and ingenious improvisation. You can't improvise with a baton, twist a modern chord out of long hair, or pluck a hot phrase out of the air with beautiful hands. These are swell things for symphony conductors to have. But a jazz orchestra, once set in motion, almost runs itself. Your job as a leader will be to drag music—not only out of the players—but out of yourself!

What is the best instrument for a bandleader to play? Does a fellow stand a better chance of success on a clarinet, say, than with a drum? Nine chances out of ten you play some instrument already. I hope so, anyway. Otherwise this book is just a cart before the horse, and I dislike putting the dollar sign in front of the musical clef.

In the selection of instruments, the beginner can

A director's dream come true! Here's an all-American swing band, representing a quarter of a million dollars worth of talent. It's a band of bandleaders. Caught by the camera in the midst of an epoch-making recording, these hard-to-get-together musicians are (l. to r.): Benny Goodman, clarinet; Eddie Miller, Toots Mondello, Benny Carter and Charlie Barnet, saxophones; extreme left, Bob Haggart, bass; second row, Charlie Christian, guitar; Jack Teagarden and Jack Jenny, trombones; rear: Gene Krupa on drums; Harry James and Charlie Spivak, trumpets. Others not encompassed

influence in some degree his chances of becoming
a leader. As a rule, I'd say that instruments you can
blow and pound are preferable to those you plunk
and scrape. In others words, wind and percussions
make better leaders' instruments than strings. For
instance, all big swing bands need a bass violin.
Yet, with the exception of John Kirby, who leads
one of the finest small aggregations in the business,
it's hard to recall a bass boss. That scarcity derives
from several good reasons. A bulky bass violin
placed in front of a band looks silly and out of
place. Furthermore, its rhythmic thump would
override the band and upset the balance of sound.
It's not a solo instrument, either in eye or ear
appeal. Even the violin may be more of a burden
than an asset for the future bandleader. A single
violin makes a band sound tinny, and only a handful of solo men have been able to extract real swing
from the instrument. Offhand, I can't think of any
big orchestra leaders who are guitar players. The
guitar ranks as a second-fiddle instrument in jazz,
though beautiful, mellow and absolutely necessary
to rhythm sections. In saying that its main object
in life is to make things comfortable for the soloist,
I don't mean to detract from the marvelous solo
guitar and ensemble work of men like Carl Kress,
Charlie Christian, George Van Epps, Allan Reuss

or Django Reinhardt. But they aren't bandleaders, and that's what we're concerned about in this book.

Judging from instrument sales, most of the young beginners are putting all their eggs in saxophones. And, providing you take up the clarinet with it, there's no better choice. On looking up the statistics on saxophones, I found that in 1937, a banner year, 40,000 saxophones were sold. At present, there are over 800,000 saxophone players in this country! That's enough to populate a city the size of St. Louis; or, by playing all at once, to depopulate a city the size of New York—in ten minutes. So, no matter what advice I offer about instruments, it looks as if Jimmy Dorsey, Charlie Barnet, Coleman Hawkins, Benny Carter and the other saxmen face some pretty hot competition.

The trombone, too, has enjoyed a terrific vogue as a bandleader's instrument. Tommy Dorsey was first on the bandwagon. Then Glenn Miller, Jack Teagarden, Bobby Byrne, Russ Morgan and Will Bradley—their trombones and their orchestras— appeared on the scene and caught on. The pianists, trumpeters and clarinetists fronting bands are too numerous to mention. And as for percussionists, Buddy Rich, Gene Krupa and the late Chick Webb drummed their way to the top; while Red Norvo,

A trio of history-makers confer at a "Metronome All-Star" recording session: (l. to r.) Nat "King" Cole, whose strange and enchanting rendition of Nature Boy swept the nation; Stan Kenton, torch-bearer of "progressive" jazz; and the trumpet trail-blazer, Dizzy Gillespie, whose bebop music somehow resembles his attire in the above photograph.

Lionel Hampton and Adrian Rollini front their own groups with marimba and vibraphone.

So, excepting the few taboo instruments I've mentioned, your choice won't be a handicap in the musical race. And remember, it's not too late to change instruments. Both Tommy and Jimmy Dorsey started out on the trumpet. They changed to trombone and sax, respectively, and play trumpet now only for a lark.

There's one thing besides musical excellence that requires stressing in this first chapter. And that's a well-rounded education. I don't mean merely the study of music theory and harmony. I mean going to school, and giving yourself an even educational break with other fellows your age. As an orchestra leader, you will appreciate the confidence which education gives you in business and social contacts. For, once at the top, you'll have to ad-lib your speeches as well as your music. Widening your knowledge and broadening your culture will also deepen the musical message you'll be able to express with your instrument. Don't forget that improvising is the same as composing, only it's done on the spot. And, in order for your composition to have form, sequence and meaning, it must first take shape as an idea in your mind. Anything you can do to enrich that mind will help in the formulation

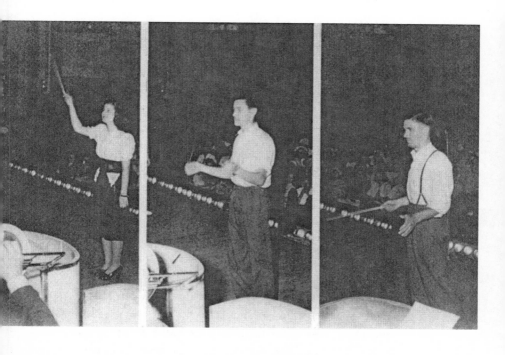

Everybody likes to lead a band, and here's the proof in pictures: Sammy Kaye, of "Swing and Sway" fame, invites amateurs to try their hand at wielding the baton on his orchestra's stage appearances.

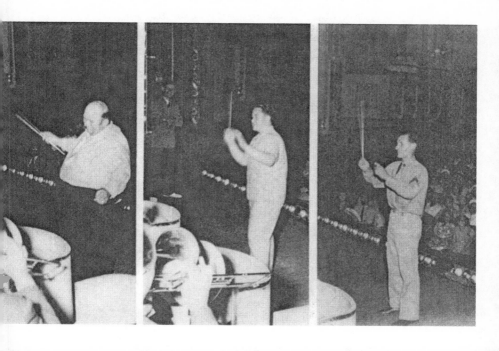

of mature and interesting musical thoughts, adding depth to whatever you create. Fletcher Henderson, whose arrangements helped popularize Benny Goodman's band, was a Phi Beta Kappa. Was it just a coincidence that Fletcher's suave arrangements caught the public's fancy and awakened America for the first time to the word "swing" and the possibilities behind it?

Well, we've taken a long running start—but that's the only kind that makes the actual jump seem simple. It's not easy money, those high stakes paid to name bands. The road up isn't paved with gold— it's only gold when you get to your destination. You can't hitch-hike or short-cut your way along. It's a stiff trudge all the way, and you follow the beaten track. If you're prepared to hoof it, come along with me and I'll try to give you some pointers to ease the way.

CHAPTER II

THE BANDLEADER MUST BE MUSICAL

AT A REHEARSAL one day, Andre Kostelanetz suddenly made an impatient gesture and halted his 45-piece orchestra in the middle of a number.

"Something's wrong with the sound of the music," he shouted.

Nobody agreed with him. Everybody thought the orchestra sounded beautiful, as always. But the maestro was disturbed. Summoning a stagehand from the wings he inquired whether anybody had tampered with the acoustically-treated walls of the studio. "No, sir, no tampering," said the stagehand. "But we did add a coat of paint." The musicians looked at each other in amazement. Only Kostelanetz had detected the muffling influence of a coat of paint on the resonance of his music. He hadn't smelled paint—he had heard it! That is what is known as an acute musical ear, and it enables Kostelanetz to stand in front of seasoned musicians and command their deep respect.

Probably the most tasteful improviser in jazz today, Teddy Wilson is an ideal model for students of modern style piano.

But don't get discouraged if you can't "hear" paint. Personally, I've never heard any in my life. A musical ear can show up in many less sensational ways. Perfect pitch—the ability to recognize any note on sound—is another rare gift. It's a nice sort of stunt to keep up your sleeve, but you can have perfect pitch and still be a pretty feeble performer as a creative musician. You can find out at psychological clinics whether you're musically hard of hearing. I'm more interested in knowing whether you've got a musical heart. There aren't any mechanical musicians among the outstanding improvisers in jazz music. An ear can make you a fine tune detective. It sifts sounds and enables you to say, "This is good," or "This is Beethoven's 'Fifth.'" Ear is what many concert-goers and critics possess—highly-sensitized ears. But playing a musical instrument with feeling, style and individuality is a question of heart and soul. Of course, you'll have to listen to music, and listen intelligently and often. But you should have the feeling that music pours into your body not through your ears—but through goose pimples. Listen to Teddy Wilson's playing of "Body and Soul" on the Goodman trio recording and decide for yourself how necessary body, heart and soul are to create a lasting chorus.

I've read fables about the phenomenal musical

talents displayed even in the cradle by successful bandleaders. There's a story that Gene Krupa always gave a steady four-four tempo on his baby rattle. Neighbors swear I used to refuse food unless it was spooned out to the tune of the "Meditation" from *Thaïs*, a habit which, at any rate, I lost later in life. Don't get panic-stricken if your mother didn't rock you to sleep with "Alexander's Ragtime Band." You can buy an instrument and start practicing with confidence of success if you're sure of just three things: you ought to know for certain that you can hum a tune; you should know without hesitation that you can hum it in key with an orchestra or piano; and you should have winced at least once in your life at the sound of a sour note or a bad chord.

Now, let's see what happens to the ear man and to the heart man when they tackle their instruments. The mechanical man becomes what is known as a "legitimate" musician, or "paperman." He reads what somebody else has written on manuscript, he blows, moves his fingers and—lo and behold—the note comes out as ordered. And it's in tune, too. The man with an ear can tell when he's sharp or flat. There's plenty of room for him in symphonies and theatre pit orchestras. Maybe he has a good tone and some slight feeling for swing-

Bud Freeman, a Whiteman alumnus, ranks among the top tenor sax men because of the novelty of his ideas and his constant striving for self-betterment.

ing something already written. In that case, he might be valuable as a section man buried in the brass or woodwinds of a modern band. But the point is he never takes a hot solo and seldom becomes a bandleader.

Your heart-and-soul man, in the meantime, has developed agility, good tone and musicianship, too. But along with that he interprets, changes the value of notes, inserts a run not in the score, buries the tune but unearths a treasure of original phrases. In short, it's mutiny against a melody, also known as improvisation.

Today's leader is often an ace improviser. He composes on his feet. He looks into space, imagines the melody in the background and embroiders a string of new notes that fit in with the harmony but weave in and out of the original melody. His ideas should be pretty and novel, or at least humorous. They must be hatched and put into action in split seconds. And musicians aren't like painters. They don't stand around a bad chord and say, "I guess that chord's all right and I'm just crazy." In music they don't hang bad chords in museums and try to stare harmony into them. A chord's either good or bad. There's no bluffing. Study them, and get as well acquainted with them as you can. Try

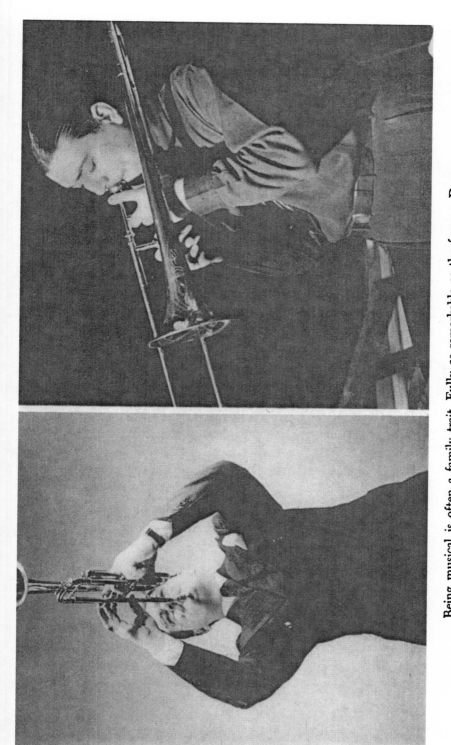

Being musical is often a family trait. Fully as remarkable as the famous Dorsey brothers are the Teagarden boys, trombonist Jackson and trumpeter Charlie.

fitting them in where they belong. For chords are the basic tools of improvisation.

Can the talent to ad-lib be acquired? Many young men have asked me where to learn improvisation. In a way that question isn't as laughable as it sounds. Strictly speaking, talent can't be picked up bit by bit along the way. The old saying about poets being born and not made also applies pretty well to musical versification. No teacher ever succeeded in turning a musical dud into anything but a showy pyro-technician. But there is one way for beginners to bring out whatever talent they may have: they must expose themselves as much as possible to fine improvisers. Their aim should be to absorb the idea and feeling behind hot style, rather than copy phrases note for note. A copied chorus is a quotation from another instrumentalist, and not improvisation. An incident in my own life demonstrates pretty well the misconception surrounding improvisation. I was in Europe for a concert tour and asked an English musician applying for a place in the orchestra, "Can you ad-lib?" "Ad-lib, sir?" responded the Englishman. "Why, I'll ad-lib anything you write."

An orchestra "swings" not because of improvisation, but because the musicians intuitively give each note a value that cannot be expressed in musical

Screen star Jane Withers shows real appreciation for Lionel Hampton's wizardry on the vibraphone.

notation. A dotted eighth note looks the same to a classical musician and to a jazz musician. Yet each gives it a distinctly different value, one old-fashioned and the other streamlined. Once that modern touch is acquired through constant listening, nothing but the sterility of your own imagination and the limitations of chord knowledge stand in the way of tasteful ad-libbing. In my opinion, everybody starts out with the old-fashioned touch. We're all born corny. A small child picking out a tune on the piano will unconsciously play more like his grandparents than like his big brother. In saying we're all born with the old-fashioned touch, I also imply that a feeling for swing can be picked up in boyhood. Before Benny Goodman conquered that corny corpuscle, Ted Lewis was his hero on clarinet. Only later did he learn to distinguish between old-time and real swing as played by men like Leon Rapollo, one of the first to play modern style clarinet.

Listening isn't enough. Some people hear music at dances, over the radio, on records and at movies, and yet remain corny all their lives. As a future bandleader you can't afford to listen half-heartedly, or with one ear. And it is important to choose your models carefully. Otherwise you might end up by improvising your way back to last century. After all, Ted Lewis takes liberties with the melody. And

Bach once improvised himself right out of a job as a church organist. But their variations—and by the way, I don't mean to class them together—have nothing in common with hot style.

What swing men can you listen to with profit? There are probably fifteen stars on each instrument, but I'll mention just a few. If you play piano, make it a habit to study Teddy Wilson, Errol Garner, Art Tatum, Earl Hines, Nat Cole, or Mel Powell. Alto saxophonists can find a variety of brilliant styles in Jimmy Dorsey, Benny Carter, Johnny Hodges (with Duke Ellington), Pete Brown and Charlie Parker. Tenor sax, probably the hottest seat in the band includes artists like Coleman Hawkins, the late Chu Berry, Ben Webster, Don Byas, Herb Haymer, Bud Freeman and Lucky Thompson. Your style-setter on trombone might be Jack Teagarden, Tommy Dorsey, Bill Harris or Brad Gowans. Roy Eldridge, Harry James, Rex Stewart, Charlie Shavers and Bobby Hackett are versatile enough to start you off right on trumpet. The swing possibilities of the guitar are brilliantly illustrated by Carl Kress, Charlie Christian, George Van Epps and Django Reinhardt. Fine clarinetists include Benny Goodman, Artie Shaw, Johnny Mince, Hank d'Amico and Buddy DeFranco. And if you play drums, you probably know the calfskin crop as well as I. For variety in styles you should pay attention to Gene Krupa, Ray Beauduc, Cozy Cole, Dave Tough, George Wettling, and Johnny Williams.

Whatever you do, don't try to learn hot licks out of a book. That's about as bad as taking a pony into a Latin exam. Any musician can spot a stolen phrase a mile away. Develop your own quirks, no matter how elementary they may be at first. Dig your ideas out of your own imagination. You can't beat the originality of a fellow in his teens. Nearly all the swing men are still using in their present style the ideas they developed when they were sixteen years old. Bix Beiderbecke played some of his most beautiful choruses when he was eighteen and nineteen. And I don't think he could ever surpass them—even if he had lived.

I've given a good deal of space to improvisation, and I'd keep at it if words could help. But there aren't any blueprints or any royal roads up the chromatic scale. If you've got your heart set on leading a band, you've got to practice with a vengeance. Your mind can be full of ideas; but without perfect mastery of your instrument, those ideas can be only imperfectly expressed. How much practice makes perfect? Four hours a day won't hurt you one bit—unless it's a question of sore lips. Frankie Trum-

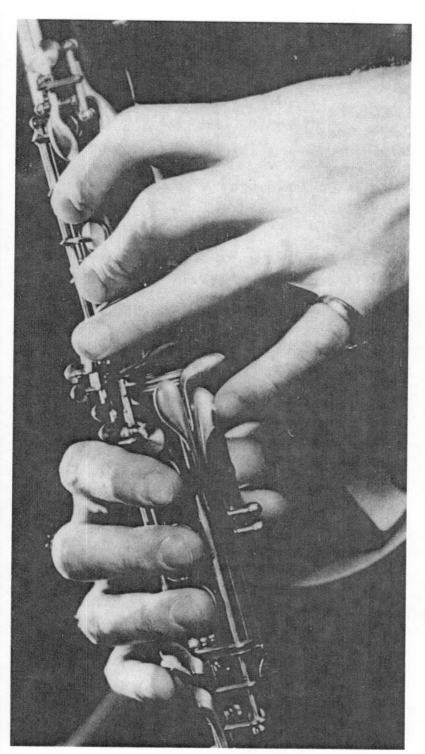

The "correct grip." It took innumerable hours of practice to give Benny Goodman's fingers their amazing dexterity.

bauer, the pioneer hot saxophonist, used to practice eight hours a day. That's why Frankie could tongue a saxophone faster than any man alive.

Finger exercises won't make you any too popular with the neighbors. It will be wise in the long run to try to put yourself in their place. Meet their complaints by closing your window. Brass instrument beginners can hang burlap in a closet and aim their horns into it. It's a nice idea every half hour or so to interrupt the technical fireworks and play a soothing Victor Herbert number. That's good neighbor-psychology. The law in some cities considers it a misdemeanor if you practice after 10 or 11 P.M., and provides for fines or jail sentences.

Music lessons are imperative. They cost money, but there's never any return without some investment. Study with experienced teachers, men who can play well enough on your chosen instrument to show its possibilities and give you something to shoot at. They don't have to be jazz musicians. In fact, it's better to take from "legit" men. You'll find later in the game that a jazz leader must be able to hold his own in classical company. Nearly all of us, for instance, have had to do a stint in theatre pit bands on the way up. Glenn Miller played "legit" in the Paramount Theatre orchestra before he became famous. Benny Goodman probably

The long-hairs and the short-hairs get together. The celebrated classical violinist, Joseph Szigeti, teams up with Benny Goodman and Bela Bartok, well-known Hungarian composer.

quaked in his boots the day John Hammond invited him to record with the high-brow Budapest String Quartet. It had to be done, though, and Goodman turned in a fine performance. Teddy Wilson feels right at home playing harpsichord duets with Yella Pessl, the country's outstanding interpreter of Bach.

Alec Templeton shows off the advantages of classical training better than anyone else I could mention. He's what I call a musician's musician and jazz can't boast many like him. Alec was born in England, which starts him right off the bat with a handicap in American swing. More than that, Templeton was blind at birth and has never seen a piano key or any other object in the world. Today Alec is one of the foremost concert pianists in America, having played with the country's principal symphonies. And he's the only person closely associated with the classics who takes rank among our hot performers. His inspired jamming in informal all-night jazz get-togethers have really been out of this world and millions have enjoyed his radio appearances. Templeton's supreme musicianship is a triumph of genius over incredible handicaps. Alec Templeton has made music live by living music.

And that can be the code of the bandleader—the bandleader you hope to be.

Alec Templeton, whom Paul Whiteman calls a complete musical genius, has musical ear-sight.

CHAPTER III

FORMING A BAND IN YOUR NEIGHBORHOOD

IT HAPPENED a few years ago at Lady Milbank's garden party in England. Hal Kemp was drinking a rather lonely spot of tea on the veranda when a stranger, in a wacky costume which included boots, sauntered up.

"Sorry to intrude, Mr. Kemp," he said. "But I've received marvelous reports about your band at the Piccadilly. Really, I'll have to come down and hear it."

"Well, now, that's just fine," Hal answered, giving the man a parting slap on the back. "Come on down, and bring the whole family."

The whole family, Hal found out later, to his discomfort, included the crowned heads of the British Empire. For the boot-shod stranger was the prince who is now King of England!

Now, what does this story have to do with forming a band in your neighborhood? Just this: Only a short time before Kemp's band attracted world-

A neighborhood band that made good: Here's the way Hal Kemp's aggregation looked when their hopes of success were still only vague dreams. The blazers, banjo, and C-Melody saxophone held by "Saxie" Dowell (second from right) are relics of a bygone age. Hal stands at extreme right. Knee-high to the bass-drum are two other modern orchestra leaders: John Scott Trotter (spectacles) now leads the band for Bing Crosby's radio show and phonograph recordings. Skinny Ennis is also well-known as a radio conductor and vocalist on the coast. Ben Williams, third from right, still plays with the Kemp band.

wide attention, it was just a pipsqueak high school outfit like thousands of others in the country today. They called themselves the "Merrymakers," and used to split $30-dance-jobs six ways. Between jobs, the Kemp band spent most of its time working out novel effects. For every hour of jobs, they practiced six. In college, later on, their distinctive style won first prize in a national amateur band contest sponsored by B. F. Keith, the vaudeville impresario. The first prize happened to be the London engagement, which incidentally put them on the map in America, too.

The neighborhood band is to swing, what the sandlot team is to major league baseball. They're the only hothouses for the breeding of young swing musicians. Playing alone all the time is exactly like talking to yourself. The first step in bandleading is learning to "converse" with other instruments, to blend in with a trio or a whole section, to soft-pedal your musical individuality for the good of the ensemble. Most of the top men started out in their local high school or town bands. As an example of how high high-school boys can graduate in music, Jimmie Lunceford was outstanding. Lunceford used to teach physical education and music at Manassa High in Memphis. There were six boys in the music class who showed special aptitude for instruments,

and Lunceford devoted all his spare time to training them in orchestra work. On their graduation,
Lunceford gave up teaching and followed his pupils
to Fisk University, where the boys received their
college education (Lunceford had graduated from
Fisk with honors a few years before). The Jimmie
Lunceford band you admired was a tribute to a
teacher's faith in his students. For it still revolved
around that original nucleus of the music teacher
and his six star pupils.

On the average, the talent available for your first
band venture won't be brilliant. The woods are full
of poor players at fourteen and sixteen—half-
hearted boys who, in the long run, will get weeded
out, sell their instruments or let them rot in the
attic. "I play sax"—these are about the easiest three
words in the musical language, because the saxophone is the easiest instrument to learn how to play
—badly. So choose your men carefully. Sort out a
few kindred spirits from your high school band.
Search around the town and corral that carpenter's
son who practices all day. Do a little eavesdropping
at the music school. Musicians are like corn on the
cob. Unless carefully hand-picked, there are lots of
bad ears.

If there's a telephone in your house and you're
willing to shoulder the burden of arranging and

postponing rehearsals—or better still, if you've got an uncle on an entertainment committee who is able to throw a couple of jobs your way—nobody will contest your right to lead the band.

Now, what instruments should this neighborhood outfit consist of? Let's not be too particular on this point. You'll be lucky if your first rehearsal doesn't turn out to be a jumble of piano, tuba, banjo, trombone, cello and bugle. No matter how good you are at anagrams you can't twist an orchestra out of that! In a small town there's only one solution: convert the tuba man into a bull fiddle player, the banjoist into a guitarist, the cellist into a saxophonist and the bugler into a trumpeter.

These switches aren't as hard as they sound. Benny Goodman's brother, Harry, started out as a tuba player. He switched to bass fiddle, though, when he found out about the tuba taboo. Benny, himself, couldn't have played with Ben Pollack or any of those early orchestras if he hadn't taken up the saxophone, which is a more basic instrument than a clarinet for a band. Once you get the group going with bona fide swing instruments, there's hardly any limit to the possible combinations. The Dorsey Brothers' orchestra, one of the finest in band history, used only one trumpet on some of their records. Yet everybody else swears by three.

Isham Jones' big organization boasted two basses—
a tuba and a bull fiddle—an unusual departure from
orthodox instrumentation. Of course, the ideal
rhythm cushion for your neighborhood band would
be piano, drums, guitar and bass violin.

But even here you can get along with all sorts of
variations. Piano and drums provided rhythm
enough for the Benny Goodman trio, and maybe it
will do for you, too. Not long ago I heard an unusual five-piece combination relying for lift on
guitar without drums. But the guitarist, instead of
beating time on the floor with his feet, converted
this waste reflex into power by pushing a regular
drummer's sock cymbal. A real five-man sextet!
Adrian Rollini's trio gets plenty of push, though
Adrian uses guitar and bass violin in place of piano
and drums. Here's a list of some outstanding small
combinations. A study of their instrumentation
might help you in organizing your neighborhood
unit.

Benny Goodman Septet—clarinet, piano, drums,
electric guitar, bass, trumpet and tenor sax.
Raymond Scott Quintet—trumpet, tenor sax,
clarinet, piano, drums and bass.
Adrian Rollini Trio—vibraphone, guitar and bass.

Clarence Profit Trio—piano, electric guitar and bass.

Bob Crosby Bobcats—trumpet, trombone, clarinet, tenor sax, piano, drums, bass and guitar.

John Kirby—trumpet, clarinet, alto sax, piano, bass and drums.

Hot Club of France Quintet—(Django Reinhardt and Stephane Grappelly) three guitars, violin and bass.

Stuff Smith—electric violin, trumpet, tenor sax, piano, guitar, bass and drums.

Big bands today often standardize their instrumentation to include four saxophones, three trumpets, two or three trombones, guitar, piano, bass violin and drums. That's the combination for you to keep in mind as your band develops.

When you start your first rehearsal get everybody around the piano and tune up. It's important to assure the best possible intonation before you begin to play at all. As a leader, one of your most important jobs is directing rehearsals. They ought to be figured out in a businesslike manner to get the most good out of each minute. Many big bands provide fines for tardiness. Union rules in New York require payment of musicians for every hour of re-

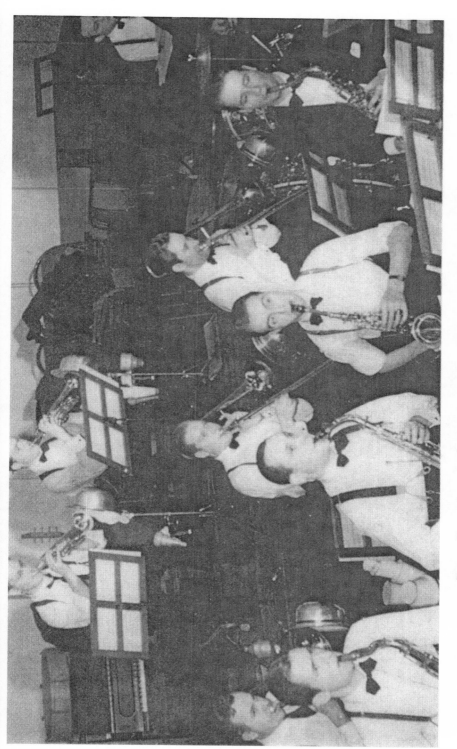

Jimmy Dorsey's orchestra rehearses for a radio program in shirt-sleeves.

hearsal time. So you can't blame the leaders for demanding attention and effort. In mammoth orchestras like mine, for instance, the rehearsal bill mounts up to staggering sums. Bandleaders are required by the union to let their men "take five"—five minutes out for a smoke—every hour. That means $130 may go up in smoke in the twelve hours of rehearsal necessary to put one half-hour radio show together. So make it a point to get down to brass tacks right from the start.

Don't waste precious moments jamming "Honeysuckle Rose." In going through a new number, it's usually best to plow through the arrangement right to the coda—despite sour notes and bewildered musicians lost along the way. This gives the band a good working idea of what comes when and where. After you've gone all the way through, then concentrate on details.

In many bigger bands you'll find section rehearsals the accepted thing. You'll find the reeds and brass off separately working on things by themselves, before or after the main rehearsal. In a band big enough to have three or four men in each section, the lead trumpet and the lead alto sax will have a great deal to do with the success or failure of their respective sections. These men must have a fine

This band's neighborhood was the house where the leader lived. Guy Lombardo's band began with four musical brothers and the quartet is still together in this picture

sense of rhythm, a good attack and a knowledge of what phrasing means. Hymie Schertzer, playing lead alto for years with Goodman's band, hardly ever took a solo. Yet the way he led the saxophone section, the fine feeling and velvety smoothness he drew out of it imparted style to the whole orchestra. Ensemble playing is a matter of teamwork, and teamwork comes only when the section leaders are on the job.

The object of rehearsals isn't to hack away like wild men at a number until it just naturally succumbs. Perfection without style is a cold and uninteresting proposition. If you don't develop a style of playing, you might end up as an orchestra leader but the orchestra will end up trailing the field. So don't forget style is your trademark, your passport to the best jobs. Fortunately, group style is easier to get than the ability of an individual to improvise. Large orchestras are branded by the peculiar arrangements they play, the tricks they use and the intonation of the instrumental combinations. Some of these musical mannerisms just develop by accident. Guy Lombardo, for instance, doesn't try to knock the slats out from under the melody. He hardly ever deviates from the tune, yet his orchestra has unmistakable trademarks. His effects come from a small subdued brass section with a dainty staccato touch, and a tearful-sounding saxophone trio with a nervous vibrato. Empty spaces in the background are filled in by delicate piano arpeggios, and the drummer is seen but not heard—by anybody except the musicians in the band.

Hal Kemp has a typical stylized band, but a lot of his effects "just grew" along the way. Hal, as you know, gets very striking results with "telegraphic trumpets" that sound like crisp dot-dash messages, and clarinets played in a broad low register inside megaphones. Vocalist Skinny Ennis is responsible for both these specialties. Rushing off the bandstand after a dance set one night, Ennis kicked a hole in the megaphone he used for singing. One of the men in the band stuck a clarinet into the megaphone and blew, fingering the instrument through the hole in the side made by Skinny's shoe. It created a brand-new sound sensation, and next day all four woodwinds were harmonizing in punctured megaphones. As for the telegraphic trumpets, they were first used merely as space-fillers behind Skinny Ennis' vocals. There was a time when Skinny couldn't hold a note more than a couple of beats —so the trumpets threw in a cascade of staccato notes to cover up the empty spaces.

If you're going to have a pure swing band, you'll have to rely on the distinctiveness of your arrangements and of your hot solo men rather than on cute tricks. It's hard to put your finger on just what makes a swing band's style. If you can describe that style, then you're describing swing! And they say that can't be done with words.

In mentioning arrangements in this chapter on neighborhood bands, I'm not suggesting that you tackle any fancy stuff. Stick to stock orchestrations until you get your bearings. Somebody in your band with arranging talent will probably volunteer a few specials. Whip them into shape and include them in your dance sets by all means . . . for that somebody in your band will soon get tired of batting out special arrangements for nothing. As a successful bandleader, you'll have to spend big money for special arrangements. That's why I say, wait until you can afford them. A musician doesn't have to be an arranger himself to lead a band. But it often eases the way to the top when the orchestra directly interprets the leader's ideas written down in black and white.

Most leaders employ a staff of arrangers and give them assignments as newspaper editors do. Some specialize in sweet numbers; others are responsible for "sock" tunes. A good arrangement costs around $200. It may be one day or two weeks in process of preparation, depending on the arranger's inspiration. Once out of the arranger's mind, the score has to be copied out on manuscript paper by union penmen—an additional forty dollars. I usually spend $1000 a week to dress up the music for just a half-hour radio show. On the other hand, the late Glenn Miller spent practically nothing but time for wonderful arrangements. For Glenn was able to combine a talent for beautifully balanced arrangements with his swell trombone playing. Larry Clinton is another bandleader who began as an arranger. Before forming his own band, Clinton did brilliant free-lance work for Tommy Dorsey and Glen Gray. Once caught in the mad rush of band-leading duties, though, there isn't much time for arranging. Even Larry Clinton and Glenn Miller farmed out much of their arranging chores.

So I'm not insisting that you arrange your own stuff. You must be able to distinguish a good arrangement from a bad one. Select the arranger who makes the band sound up to your ideals. Guide him with suggestions if you want, trim a measure here and spruce up a passage somewhere else. But rely on a specialist for arrangement output. You'll have your hands full rehearsing the band, playing your instrument, and taking care of the thousand-and-one little problems that only the bandleader can cope with.

We've been talking big in this chapter on neighborhood bands. High-sounding stuff . . . special arrangements, style, instrumentation and rehearsals. Problems of the future, perhaps. But the germ of special arrangements, the germ of style and everything else I've mentioned should already be at work even in your miniature band beginnings.

There's one thing the boys will have to do like full-fledged professionals—that's play a dance job. When you start to play dance music remember one thing—people want to dance. If people come to hear you because they know your style of playing and like it, you can wander off a bit, but on your first engagement deliver what they've ordered—music to dance by.

It may seem like ABC to say that you should check the attire of the bandsmen before you get to the job. Be sure every one of them looks like the kind of young man you would like to have in your own home. And try to see that every band member acts like the kind of fellow that deserves to be asked back again.

Don't let on that this is one of your first jobs. The people on the floor may not know much about a saxophone, but they're awfully good at recognizing a greenhorn. Introducing new members of the band to each other in full view on the stand is bad

Here's a neighborhood band that hit the high seas in summer. They look corny all right, but you can blame the pose on the ship's photographer. Since these days of glory, the "Paris" has gone down, the trombonist has become a G-Man, the cornetist manufactures candy, the guitarist sells Wheaties, the pianist has a newspaper job in Walla Walla, Washington, and the saxophone player collaborates on books with Paul Whiteman.

Paul Whiteman, Jr. played this set of drums in his own neighborhood combination.

psychology. Bands are hired because they're supposed to be old hands at playing together. So if there are any new recruits, postpone the handshaking until first intermission.

Select your dance sets to please the guests and not the musicians. Play a rhumba, a waltz or a tango every two sets even if it kills you. Kicking off the right dance tempo will be one of your severest tests. Failure to set a natural pace might turn your debut into a swan song. Avoid sudden accelerations and changes of tempo, showy devices suitable only for stage appearances. And when the job is over, make a discreet attempt to collect the money on the spot. The music boss has a pay-envelope responsibility towards his men. They have a right on these single jobs to be paid in cash. Checks are usually greeted with wry faces—especially if it's Saturday night and the job pays only five dollars.

As a bandleader, you'll have to smile in the face of such things as these: your best girl dances all night with your worst rival; a boisterous couple knocks three or four music stands over without apologizing; the whole room acts noisy and oblivious while you play your most beautiful choruses; somebody requests "Star Dust" just one second after you played it. Plaster a smile on your face and keep it there despite everything!

Now that you've got the feel of a band and the taste of a job, you've got a right to wonder what comes next. Say good-bye to your neighborhood. You're on your way up to Big Time!

A diplomatic ruler of men makes friends in every field. Here's Mark Warnow, famous radio conductor, being treated to a complimentary meal at the Automat by CBS page boys.

CHAPTER IV

THE BANDLEADER MUST BE A DIPLOMATIC RULER OF MEN

HARDLY a day goes by that the boss doesn't light into the tenor sax player. Right now he's assuming his Little Napoleon pose again. Feet braced wide apart, hands on his hips, the leader fixes an accusing glare on his pet scapegoat.

"Did you hit that sour note, Smith?" he roars.

But for some reason Smith doesn't give his usual meek and evasive answer. Something that must have smoldered inside him for a long time suddenly bursts into flame. With slow dramatic movements he sets his saxophone on the chair and then strides savagely to the front.

"No, Mr. Blank," he yells. "Smith did *not* hit that sour note but . . . (biff) . . . Smith's going to hit one awfully sour guy . . . (biff) . . . so hard he'll . . . (biff) . . . never forget it . . ." (flop).

In other words, a bandleader must be a diplomatic ruler of men—or else!

Getting hit in the jaw isn't the worst thing that

can happen to the bandleader who is a bully. After all, a musician knows he may have to pound the pavements for weeks in search of another job. And of the two, the conductor can get along with his shiner lots better than the sax man can stand a black eye up at union headquarters. Consequently, grudges seldom come to blows in the music game. The disliked leader's worst nightmare is sabotage: fifth column activities by the second trumpet, third sax and first trombone. Instead of playing their best, the men do a half-hearted job, giving their boss the instrumental bird here and a Bronx-cheer effect there. A band that dislikes the leader can usually manage to make the public dislike the band. That's why the best bands are made up of men who are good friends, and that's why no bandleader will ever last on top unless he's genuinely friendly with his boys.

Now the first thing to remember as head man is that each musician is a temperamental little artist in his own right—or at least in his own mind. And considering the fact that he's a pretty sensitive sort of chap—already forced to abide by the laws of his country, the laws of his conscience and the laws of the musicians' union—he won't appreciate having to take orders from another policeman at rehearsals. I think there's something symbolical about the fact

A historic photograph of neighborliness among bandleaders. Here's the late Glenn Miller, welcomed back to the Paramount Theatre by four friendly rivals who led his band when illness temporarily put Glenn out of the running. The four are Tommy Dorsey, Gene Krupa, Dick Stabile and Charlie Barnet.

that swing bandleading doesn't require a stick. It seems to give expression to the idea that this new kind of music is free and loose and has no need of the dictator or any of his affectations.

Whatever you do, don't humiliate a musician in front of his colleagues. When somebody hits a bad note twice at the same spot—which indicates the cause is more permanent than just a fly wandering over the score—you might stop the band and say, "Boy, who hit that clinker!" But don't wait for an answer or look in the direction where things sounded suspicious.

I'm not trying to compile a dictionary of don'ts in this chapter. But there is one more thing I'd like to warn against, and that's the mistake some leaders make of requiring a musician to run through a difficult passage alone while his associates sit around and gape at him. You might as well crown him with a dunce cap. Squawking at individuals should take place backstage. Praise, on the other hand, has its strongest effect when bestowed in front of the whole band.

If you're angry, rant against everything in general but nobody in particular. Toscanini, for instance, is noted for his outbursts of fury. But he takes his tantrums out on inanimate objects and not on human beings. He's liable at rehearsals suddenly to whisk all his music onto the floor, kick his music stand off the stage, break his baton and throw the pieces. But before throwing, Toscanini whips around like a baseball pitcher trying to catch a man off second base and lets fly behind him into an empty hall. He learned from a trumpeter in the New York Philharmonic not to make personal attacks on musicians. It was shortly after Toscanini arrived in America for the first time. For several rehearsals the eminent conductor had been picking on Harry Glantz, the Philharmonic's first trumpeter, who is one of the top men in the whole world. The "old man"—the name applied to all classical leaders behind their backs—still unfamiliar with English, used to administer all his tongue-lashings in Italian. Finally Glantz got sore at always being the butt of Toscanini's wrath and stalked off the stand. As the trumpeter neared the door, Toscanini, white with rage, tried to wither him with one last torrent of words. With his hand already on the door-knob, Glantz glanced around and faced the boss.

"Nuts to you," he said calmly.

"Oh no, oh no," Toscanini screamed in faltering English. "It is too late now—to apologize."

Toscanini's English had suddenly turned the whole affair into a huge joke—on himself. Somebody close to him whispered the meaning of "nuts to you" in Italian and the maestro broke down and joined in the laughter. Since then, though, he has steered clear of verbal clashes.

Nobody would ever try to run a modern dance band with all the pomp and discipline used in symphonies. For instance, probably half of the men in the NBC Symphony, though members for several years, have never spoken with Toscanini. In rehearsals, they address him respectfully as "maestro." He calls the men by their last names. But first he finds out what that is, by consulting a seating chart glued to his podium. Returning from a vacation, he strides onto the stage while the orchestra stands at attention. Unlike some of his less formal colleagues, he wastes no time relating holiday experiences. His first words after a long absence are, "Good afternoon. Let us begin with 'Tannhaüser.'" A chance meeting in the elevator between Toscanini and a handful of his musicians is usually a sign for the men to step out and allow the maestro to travel solo. Once in a while, tokens of esteem do pass between them. At Christmas, the members of the orchestra chip in on gifts like beautiful gold cuff links for the boss. Mr. and Mrs. Toscanini give each man, say, a tie and a tie-clip with "Toscanini" engraved on it. One time on the maestro's birthday the orchestra, assembled in rehearsal hall, got Toscanini at home on

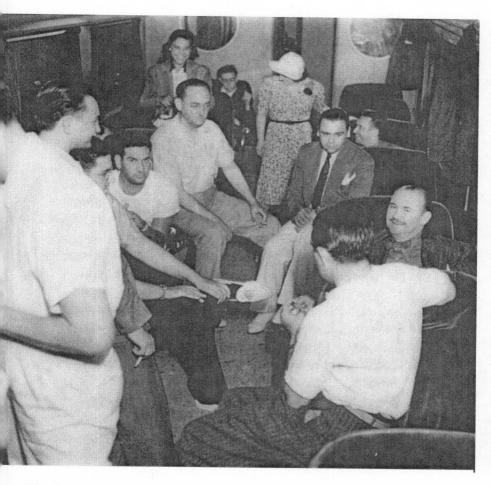

The band and the boss go over the bumps together. Traveling
between jobs isn't always fun, but Paul Whiteman's endless store
of anecdotes helps relieve tedium.

the phone and played "Happy Birthday to You" while the distinguished conductor listened at the receiver. The orchestra later learned indirectly that the maestro had been deeply touched.

Your jazz band leader isn't on such a high perch. Jealousies and bickerings among boys in the band affect him directly and call for his personal intervention. His musicians come to him to ask for a raise, a loan, or advice on family affairs. They enlist him to serve as best man at their weddings, name him godfather to their children, and select him as a pallbearer at their mother-in-law's funeral. The leader is a buddy. Yesterday he was just one of the boys, and he doesn't forget how that feels. He still sits with them at lunch counters, he travels over the same bumps and tosses on the same kind of mattress as the rest of the band. For summer travel he keeps up the general morale by insisting on air-cooled coaches for his orchestra. Over-night hauls in buses are taboo, despite the savings in money. Hotel reservations are made in advance so the men don't have to shift for themselves and risk bad accommodations. Even in apparent trivialities like allotting upper and lower berths, the orchestra chief, through his manager, bears a heavy responsibility. A first-come-first-served system would probably result in nightly free-for-alls. Our band manager distributes

This is Casa Loma, Inc. Glen Gray, who was actually elected head of the band by a show of hands, has incorporated the whole outfit.

lower berths only to band veterans. Mike Pingitore, who many years ago arrived at the first rehearsal ten minutes before me, gets the easiest-riding lower berth right in the center of the car. Upper berths are assigned to newer members, and rookies sleep in the end ones right over the wheels.

Bandleaders often sacrifice money and jobs for the sake of the orchestra's morale. When banjoist Pingitore's son was near death up in Minnesota; we broke up our act so "Goldy," the band's comedian-trumpeter, could make a rush trip to donate blood for a transfusion. That sacrifice gave a new lease on life to the Pingitore boy, earned Goldy a deeper affection among the men, and brought us all closer together. In the same vein, Glen Gray had his band incorporated, which means that everybody can share equally in its operation and profits.

From the musical standpoint, one of the band-leader's most diplomatic jobs is assigning solos. Plenty of good outfits include not one, but two or three men who are whizzes, say, on trumpet. Maybe one stands out slightly above the others and his sensational choruses might be one reason for the band's success. You'd like to give this man a monopoly on all the hot trumpet choruses—but don't do it! Ration the spotlight and keep peace in the band. At one time Benny Goodman had a battery of three of the country's finest improvisers on trumpet—Harry James, Chris Griffen and Ziggy Elman. James happened to get most of the solo assignments. But the other men were too exceptional to be left out in the cold, and Goodman had to keep the score as even as possible. This was done by letting Ziggy and Chris each make a whole record on which each was featured. "Zaggin' with Zig" was Ziggy Elman's private number. His name went on the record and nothing was allowed to detract from his playing. On the recording of "Young Man with a Horn," the only noticeable horn was blown by Chris Griffen, who made up for lost time.

Practically all this advice about getting along with musicians could be summed up by—have a heart! Leave browbeat out of your downbeat. Old Tom Brown used to wear kid gloves when he played the saxophone. And that's what you ought to wear when you lead a band!

CHAPTER V

THE BANDLEADER MUST BE A SHOWMAN

ONCE, long ago, court musicians used to march into tournament arenas proudly leading the parade of knights in armor. All eyes in the bloodthirsty grandstands would be fastened on the warriors, girded for life-and-death jousts with spears. The poor musicians, for all their fanfare, hardly had a look-in. Whatever attention they managed to steal resulted from the showiness of their costumes, a ripple of applause being the usual reward for the fellows who strutted around in the gaudiest jackets and the niftiest kilts.

Since those old days, interesting changes have taken place in the world. Knightly tournaments have gone out of fashion. And people's ears have improved immensely, while their eyes have become weakened to such an extent that practically everybody needs glasses to see what's going on. Radio has turned the world into a big blind audience, and the amount of beauty our ears can absorb is increas-

84

ing in every way. But people are still unable to make
a meal of unadulterated music! Some of the old
craving for pomp and panoply lingers on. And the
orchestra that goes under the assumption that music
alone can sell a band will go under. Unless you can
dramatize your music, you may even have trouble
competing with inferior organizations—orchestras
that put up a glamorous front and specialize in
showmanship.

Now, showmanship's an awfully hard word to pin
down. Showmanship, I'd say, is the art of making
difficult things look easy and easy things look impossible. When the shortstop stands still for a pop
fly and catches it with one hand, that's showmanship. He made it look hard. When he has to run a
mile into left field with his back to the ball, and
then suddenly plants himself and nabs the ball
easily with two hands—that, besides being a good
catch, also has the effect of good showmanship. He
accomplished with ease what had seemed an impossibility.

Playing trumpet was always second nature to
Charlie Teagarden, and he never saw any point in
trying to make it look like a stunt. But Hollywood
changed his opinions on that score. The directors
wanted showmanship. They wanted him to make
faces when he played a hot lick, as if he were pull-

ing a tree up by its roots. They wanted him to sway
back and forth, aim the trumpet like an anti-aircraft
gun at the sky and make little gyrations so that
the bell of the instrument wrote invisible messages
in the air. That, believe it or not, is what the public
wants. It's the jazz equivalent of Menuhin's swaying body and unruly hair. It appeals to the man in
the audience who doesn't know a thing about music,
but who thinks he recognizes a difficult feat when
he sees one.

But don't be too quick to belittle Hollywood's
influence on musicians and bandleaders. The op-
portunities offered by the movies to photogenic orchestras are really limitless. A big bandleader recently got $25,000 for a part in a super-film.
Hollywood gossip columns are brimming over with
the doings of musical big-shots. As is well known,
Harry James, Xaviar Cugat and Tommy Dorsey
have all journeyed to the film capital to appear in
feature-length movies. Orrin Tucker and Andre
Kostelanetz have worked on the Paramount lot. Bob
Crosby's outfit was on location with RKO's *Malvina
Swings It*. Freddie Martin has made shorts for
Warner Brothers, as most of the great bands have
already done at some time or other. Our orchestra
once made a picture with Judy Garland and Mickey
Rooney; and Artie Shaw has invaded Hollywood

also. That gives you an idea of what Hollywood means to bands—and why bands need showmanship.

Showmanship shouldn't be confused with style. Style, which we talked about in the last chapter, is the personality of the band as expressed in its music. Showmanship is the way the music is presented, the costumes and the mannerisms of the musicians who play it. It isn't as artistic or as subtle a thing as style. Like varnish, you can lay it on in any thickness. It's usually the creation not of the bandleader but of his publicity man and business manager. Showmanship helps turn music notes into banknotes, and you need it in your band!

The name of your outfit, while not the most important factor in showmanship, can actually contribute to, or injure your chances of, success. For instance, if you're Archibald Przasnyaz or anything like that, something ought to be done. Some names need pruning down, some a manicure, others a complete alteration. One of the identifying marks of today's topnotchers is their habit of using the diminutive form of their first names whenever possible. For example, take Jimmy Dorsey, Eddy Duchin, Bobby Byrne, Sammy Kaye, Charlie Ventura Tommy Dorsey, Herbie Kay, Johnny Messner, Woody Herman, Artie Shaw and Freddie Martin. I don't know where Benny Goodman would have ended up as Benjamin or even Ben Goodman. Names like Robert, Arthur, and so on almost invariably revert to corresponding nicknames with "y" or "ie" added just to make them a little more down-to-earth. Classical conductors cling to their formal and more solemn monickers, and they like them foreign-sounding, if possible. In swing, these gentlemen would have to transpose themselves into Artie Toscanini, Leo Stokowski and Johnny Barbirolli. Names, in every walk of entertainment life, can help you sink or swim. So when you choose a name, remember you're marrying the band to it.

Many groups use two names, the name of the leader plus a subtitle, like the old dime-novel thrillers. For example, there's Woody Herman and the Band That Plays the Blues. In such cases, the first name is like the family name, and the one tacked on is "given" by the press agent or manager. This glued-on name is the one that may either be very showmanly or very corny. Name styles have changed, and you've got to be careful in your selection. For example, Cab Calloway used to call his band "The Missourians." Coon-Sanders were the "Kansas City Night Hawks." Tommy and Jimmy Dorsey got their start with the "Scranton Sirens." Nowadays these sound more like baseball teams, especially when

They thought this idea was corny until Glenn Miller revived it.
Actually, the brass hats, besides providing colorful tonal effects,
keep onlookers interested in the proceedings.

Carlton Coon of Coon-Sanders called himself "the old left-hander."

But if you ever hope to be booked into places like the New Yorker or the Congress Hotel in Chicago, avoid descriptives like "The Merrymakers," "The Jazz Hounds," and so on. The power of a band's name is sometimes a good deal more decisive than its music. A young friend of mine played his way over to Europe on a steamer about four years ago. His band was called the "Washington Musical Ambassadors," after Washington University in St. Louis, where the boys attended college. The Europeans, however, thought from the name that the orchestra had been sent over as ambassadors of goodwill by the government in Washington, D. C. Wherever they traveled on the continent, these amateur musicians were treated almost like accredited diplomats. That's what's in a name!

Lately a few bands have been very successful with names like "Champagne Rhythm," "Rippling Rhythm," "Tic-Toc Rhythm" and other mysterious rhythms. Judging from their popularity with a specialized public there will always be room at the top for a handful of them.

The dictionaries are wide open for young bandleaders with a flair for showmanship. Some very good bands do add box-office appeal through use of high-sounding phrases like Jimmie Lunceford's "School of Jazznocracy," signifying nothing. But maybe it helps sell the band to people who wouldn't ordinarily listen to something as drab-sounding as "swing." "Glen Gray and His Casa Loma Band" sounds swell and packs a load of showmanship. Just because it sounds good, nobody gives a hang about the meaning. If anybody did, he might have wondered long ago about "Glen Gray and His *Mud House* Orchestra."

Individual titles of King of This and Dictator of That are yours for the asking. Consequently they've become almost valueless, and have little showmanship punch. Charlie Barnet, Coleman Hawkins, Jimmy Dorsey, Dick Stabile and Herbie Fields are often billed by their managers as either King, Dictator or World's Greatest saxophonist. Benny Goodman picked up the title, "King of Swing," somewhere along the way and I guess several other musicians are called the same thing. It's all very impressive, provided the radio audience doesn't hear the claims of four Kings in one night. If you can think of anything new to be King of, though, snatch at it, by all means. Be sure though you choose a title for which you will not be sued. I was the first claimant to the title "King of Jazz," yet I was sued by a Philadelphia musician who claimed he had patented himself "The Jazz King."

Stage and screen appearances put a big premium on visual showmanship, and your neighborhood dances require it in small doses. Some bands employ interior decorators to work out attractive stage settings. A rich blending of spotlights on a brilliant array of instruments, set off against an original backdrop, adds luster to the music.

Even small items like music-stands offer wide possibilities for variation. You won't find two orchestras in the country using stands identical in shape and color. Some of the pictures in this book provide a good cross section of music-stand styles. Nearly all of them bear the initials of the conductor. Yet the style of lettering is never the same. Some bandleaders have scenes painted on the music desks. There were camels on Bob Crosby's, and modernistic designs of musical instruments on Glenn Miller's. Goodman tried something new by stamping each stand not only with a big B.G., but with the names of the individual instrumental stars who sat behind them. Maybe what your band needs is one bang-up carpenter.

The unison swaying of whole sections of the orchestra in time with the music was always classed

A lesson in visual showmanship by one of the historic bands of all times. Bob Crosby's old Dixieland band appealed to the eye (and the sponsor) with camel-studded music stands. Notice, too, the attractive modernistic designs of musical instruments in the background.

as grandstand play before Glenn Miller made it part of his stage routine. Now several bands have revived it. Brass hats catching the glint of the spotlight, swift dramatic changes of mutes by the trumpets, a lightning switch from saxes to clarinets in the woodwinds, mass movements of complete sections to the front of the stage to get a good microphone pick-up—these are all musical necessities which can be turned to good account theatrically. There's hardly a band that doesn't try to put on some sort of spectacle. Even Guy Lombardo uses a museum-piece instrument that is halfway between a harpsichord and a zither, plus a mellophone—both effective pieces of visual showmanship because they look strange. I hardly need mention Gene Krupa's remarkable flair as a showman. Luckily, he happens to be a genius with the drums. Otherwise Gene's gyrations and ferocious faces might be resented by musicians. In general, the boys will excuse the hokus-pokus stuff if there's real talent behind it. If not, giving yourself airs won't be necessary—you'll get the air soon enough!

The drapery, backdrop, and the instruments' glare all form part of the spectacle you try to create. But while draperies help make the act, clothes make the men in the band. Now, by clothes and costumes I don't mean men in uniform, so much as men uni-

Even Lombardo resorts to tricks of showmanship. This midget
"harpsichord" with a charming tinkle and a provocative appearance
attracts a lot of attention.

formly dressed. The official wardrobe usually includes about two outfits. Each one sets the individual band members back about eighty-five dollars apiece. A boss who required more than two big outlays for clothes a year would find his musicians moping around with long faces—which, on the stage, means being short on showmanship.

Les Brown's crew, a sort of Beau Brummel model for college bands, wears plain tuxedo for hotel dates as a background to Les' tails. On the stage the musicians sport a green summer formal attire with maroon bow ties. Les stands in front of the band in midnight-blue trousers plus a light tan summer-formal coat.

Stay conservative in clothes. Insist on neatness and uniformity, but steer clear of thick braid, military epaulettes and doormen's costumes.

One of the best ways of giving visual "it" to a band is to use a girl vocalist. Put yourself in the place of the audience or the guests at a dance. Looking at the bandstand, they see nothing but a monotonous row of tuxedo on tuxedo. No man is glamorous blowing a horn, and when there's a battalion of them on the dance floor horizon all evening, no one but a musician is likely to take two looks. A male singer only makes matters worse. That's why almost every successful bandleader these

A girl vocalist sharpens the band's appearance. Here's Martha Tilton, who since has branched out on her own, singing with Benny Goodman's orchestra. Notice the transparent glass weights which keep the musical scores from going with the wind.

days primps up the bandstand with at least one pretty girl. To spectators she's like a melody, and if she can sing one, so much the better. It'll send your stock soaring with both the girls and the men in your audience. It's sex appeal for one and clothes appeal for the other, the size and originality of a songstress' wardrobe being very important. I've made it a practice to use girl vocalists in my orchestra wherever possible, not for showmanship reasons alone, but because feminine vocalists are tops in swing interpretation. Mildred Bailey, Ella Fitzgerald, Billie Holiday, Dinah Shore, Peggy Lee and a host of others have backed male singers right off the map. So add variety and another pinch of showmanship by putting an angel in among your swing stars.

There are many more ways than I've mentioned for novel presentation of your band. It's up to you to choose the best sort of showmanship. Be sure it's not just show-off. New tricks of showmanship are being invented all the time and depend a lot on the personality of the individual bandleader. Kay Kyser has turned his Southern accent into a very attractive asset. Ben Bernie's "I hope you like it" and his reference to himself as the "Old Maestro" were almost as important as his music to people listening in. Ted Lewis' high hat and his "Is Everybody Happy?" will be memories a lot longer than his clarinet. Another band grew famous on the radio partly because of its leader's distinctive way of saying, "Lopez speaking." Sammy Kaye and a couple of other bands attracted attention with singing titles. Everybody else simply announced the name of the song. But, in the Kaye band, the vocalist sang the title during the first few bars of the arrangement. That's salesmanship, showmanship, good merchandising or whatever you want to call it.

Only I hope with all my heart that as a leader you concentrate on music and not on building better mouse-traps—or Mickey-Mouse bands. Let your publicity man dream up the bag of tricks. Be prepared to veto most of them. But try to retain enough of the non-musician's mentality to recognize the kind of showmanship that will sell your band not only to musicians, but to lawyers, debutantes, doctors, housewives, accountants, store clerks, taxi drivers, college students and stenographers. When you've entertained all of them, you're more than a musician—you're a showman!

CHAPTER VI

GETTING A JOB

THE road to success is paved with jobs. But the hardest job of all is to find work. Failure in that search has wrecked hundreds of fine young bands. Joblessness has also caught up with established musical organizations, causing sudden upsets and disbandments. Hundreds of ex-leaders now play in radio and theater pit orchestras, victims of their inability to find work for their own aggregations.

Music is fun. But the finest music, the closest friendships and the firmest resolve to reach the top aren't enough to hold a band together. Morale can't buy bread and support families, and "fun" isn't a weekly pay check. The members of an orchestra look to the leader for steady employment. If they can't get it with one leader, they'll drift away to another. Showmanship, style and arrangements can be picked up along the way. But jobs are a matter of the moment. They have to start early in a band's history and continue with regularity all down the

The history of jazz down through the years is written in the face of
W. C. Handy and in his most memorable composition—The St.
Louis Blues. Here the venerable father of the blues is shown with the
outstanding orchestra leader of the 20th century—Duke Ellington.

line. You can't hand the boys in the band a tele-
scope and say, "See that speck way off there on the
horizon—well, that's your next job." Earlier in this
book I said you shouldn't be hungry for fame and
fortune. That doesn't mean you and your boys
should *go hungry*. Being practical is not the same
thing as greediness. None of the great musical ears
are entirely deaf to the jingle of coin, and that goes
for the highest and mightiest in both the classical
and jazz fields. A pay check is the most beautiful
piece of manuscript ever set before a musician. It
enables him to support himself and his family. It
makes it possible for him to follow music as a profession.

The bandleader's approach in getting a job differs
from that used in almost any other calling. He can't
open a newspaper and find opportunity on the clas-
sified-ad page. Unlike a doctor, a printer, a lawyer, an
architect and other specialists, the music man can't
apprentice or interne himself to well-established
specialists, whom he later replaces. His vocabulary
doesn't even include the words, "Give me a job."
Why? Because the bandleader is looking for fourteen jobs. He sells in carload lots. Unlike the majority of job-hunters, he can't afford to accept low
wages in return for "a wonderful future." The group
he represents might disagree about what constitutes

a rosy future. But they'd surely recognize a financial fizzle on sight. Your "salary requirements," as
the phrase goes, will sound like war-debt install-
ments. They're the kind of figures that frighten
prospective employers. Just for fun I figured out
recently about how many packages of cigarettes one
of the large manufacturers had to sell per year to
pay the band that advertised its product over the
radio. Well, it took a neat 5,200,000 packages to do
the trick. That isn't chicken feed. A band's upkeep
doesn't always necessitate such a tremendous turn-
over in its employer's merchandise. But whether you
work for a man who sells tickets on a dance floor or
automobiles for the highway, his volume of business
must be primed for large outlays. Hiring a band is a
big deal. It requires close figuring and expense jug-
gling. That's why your lot as a job-seeker will be
tougher than the fellow who hunts alone. He can
be an employee, but you are an investment.

And the trouble is you're seldom a long-term investment. In radio, for example, band contracts
usually run for only thirteen weeks. At the end of
that time, the sponsors can renew the contract. On
the other hand, they're perfectly free to let the band
go. Single theater engagements tide the band over a
week or, at the most, three weeks. At a hotel, the
musicians' residence might stretch out to a couple

In twenty years Paul Whiteman has traveled millions of miles to fill the nation's highest jobs. Music, too, has traveled far but no orchestra has moved more smoothly with the times than the aggregation whose amazing development is shown on this page. Mike

Pingitore, the little banjoist who sits at the extreme right of the 1919 picture, is the only original member left in the band today. By virtue of an early arrival at the first rehearsal, he has been in the orchestra longer than Whiteman himself.

of months. And I don't have to tell you how long an "overnight stand" lasts.

The head man of a band has to consider each job a jumping-off place, every bandstand a fishing ground for future engagements. Trombonist Tommy Dorsey, before he became a leader, was employed by twenty-two different bands in a single year. Now, as a boss in his own right, he might work for that many employers over a stretch of a month or two. Only a few exclusive night clubs in New York place orchestras on anything resembling a permanent basis. And these are spots where music is a background for conversation and not a subject of conversation in itself. Eddie Davis, with twelve years running as orchestra leader at Larue's, a swank night club and eating place, holds some sort of longevity record for New York.

Looking out for the future doesn't mean being half-hearted or disloyal in the job of the moment. Every director uses his sponsor's product and puts his whole heart into delivering the promised musical goods. But he owes it to himself and to his musicians to provide for tomorrow. Orchestras, like any business concern, depend not on a week's or a month's bonanza, but on a steady flow of money into the treasury. They need some spares in the bank in case of a flat week.

Now there's no trick to getting your first job. It will probably be a picnic or a Sunday school dance, with wages consisting literally of ice cream and cake. If there's chocolate sauce on the ice cream, why, that's all gravy. Many successful bands accepted their first job on just such a barter system— exchanging music for refreshments and a chance to be heard by their teachers, school friends and parents. Ice cream and cake can usually be found at the first rung of every success ladder.

The next step is a job that pays two dollars per man. This may be a Saturday night dance at the neighborhood church, a high school fraternity function or the social aftermath of a basketball game. The mechanics behind these jobs is simple. Somebody on the entertainment committee happened to hear your music at the ice-cream social; or maybe heard about it second-hand from a friend who was there. Anyway, the mad whirl of Saturday night jobs is on. Somebody else, from the opposite side of town, hears the band and hires it for regular Wednesday night dances. Your reputation trickles into other neighborhoods and becomes something for near-by bands to compete with.

In the summertime, there's a job at a resort lodge in the mountains. You play for room and board and five dollars apiece per week. Two college students, a president of a country club, three sub-debutantes, and an assistant hotel manager from your home town spend a few days of the summer at your resort. The following winter, that nets you five fraternity dances, two coming-out parties, Thanksgiving, Christmas and New Year's Eve jobs at the country club, plus an engagement for the Elks' Ball in your city's largest hotel. Your men collect between four and seven dollars now for an evening's work. As time goes by, the band develops flash and style and plays smoothly as a unit. The chance comes up for a steady job as the hotel's regular dance band. And then suddenly comes your first experience with— the union.

Nobody who isn't a member of the American Federation of Musicians can take a steady job, play in theaters, hotels, in movies or over the radio. Joining that protective organization is an absolute necessity for the members of your band. Every jazz musician in every orchestra heard or seen in the entertainment field must belong to it. The advantages of membership will be of inestimable value to your group. The union's aim is to protect the musicians' interests. Wherever one of the 750 local chapters exists, you find higher wages, shorter hours and better working conditions for the people in the profession. Before Local 10 got under way in Chicago,

Here's a bandleader radio made. Raymond Scott was a pianist on the CBS Saturday *Night Swing Session* before organizing his quaint quintet, predecessors of this band.

for example, men in pit bands used to draw around twelve dollars a week. Now they earn ninety-nine dollars.

Many new bands have a wrong impression about the union. It stands athwart their path, and keeps them from taking a steady job. But some day, when music is your business, you'll understand the union's actions. Its job is to shield the men who rely solely on music for their livelihood. The services of a high school band can be bought cheaply. What would happen to the professional musician if he were forced to compete in a price-war with youngsters who love to play and, what's more, have parents to support them? To guard against this conflict between professionals and amateurs, the union fixes a minimum scale to fit every establishment. The minimum varies from city to city, but it always provides a fair return for the work given. When your band is ready to take a regular job, music has ceased to be just a pastime and has become a serious business. That's where the union comes in, and that's where you go in the union. Initiation fees range from fifty to a hundred dollars. But don't forget a union musician is reimbursed for that outlay by his first week's salary. In addition to this initial payment, there are yearly dues of around fifteen dollars.

Many's the time I've thanked the AFM for

fighting the musician's battle. The union will help you, too, in your struggle toward the top. There are no two ways about it. Getting your band the jobs that count means joining the Musicians' Union.

Your union outfit is eligible now for all approved local jobs. That means you can accept the hotel "date" as a steady proposition. During the summer lay-off, you can coast profitably along into other jobs on the hotel publicity. A local booker may arrange for several one-night stands in country dance halls. Loud posters herald your arrival weeks in advance. Some of the overnight jumps cover one or two hundred miles. In one of the towns, you play opposite a famous New York aggregation. Some of their boys hang around and seem to like the way your band sounds. Promising to put in a good word with a mammoth Broadway booking agency, these traveling musicians are the first to carry your name to the heart of the entertainment world. Nearly all important bands are handled by booking organizations like the Music Corporation of America, Consolidated Radio Attractions, William Morris, and the General Amusement Corporation. They book bands all over America, but they don't waste time with second-rate or unprofitable outfits. It's good for ambitious orchestras in outlying districts to have an interested spokesman in New York or Chicago.

Sending private recordings—which can be made cheaply in almost any large-sized town—is a good way to bridge the distance between your band and the important men who must hear it.

Try, above all else, to get your hotel, night club or dance hall to broadcast a half-hour of your music nightly. An air program, even local, is often the opening wedge to national prominence. A radio wire represents a negligible cost to a hotel, and usually brings in more dollars than it removes from the till. If your local station happens to be a network outlet, the band stands the chance of overnight recognition. During Howard Hughes' Round-the-World flight, for instance, CBS stayed open all night. In the wee hours of the morning, things in New York were pretty dead. So the network pulled in unknown orchestras playing at night spots in the Midwest and on the Coast. A network official listening in happened to like the work of two of these bands, and a little later offered them the greatest publicity any band can hope for—a half-hour broadcast of dance music over a nation-wide hookup three times a week. Recently, too, when the New York Musician's Local 802 placed a temporary ban on broadcasting orchestra music, networks had to fall back on offerings by out-of-town stations. That emergency brought to the fore Joey Kearns, a bandleader on

WCAU, Philadelphia, the station that also gave
Jan Savitt his start. So keep that mike handy. Even
if the local station isn't hooked up with a network,
there's always the chance that some touring im-
presario might pick up your band on his car radio
as he drives along in the night.

Be sure you understand the restrictions clamped
on out-of-town musicians before striking out for
New York. Remember the local union's first duty
is to protect members against the encroachment of
musicians from other cities. An out-of-town musician finds himself in much the same position as an
alien. Before reaching an equal footing with local
musicians, he has to "take out his first papers." That
means establishing a residence for a period of six
months or so, during which time he cannot accept
a steady position. Probation over, the "citizenship
papers" are handed out and the outsider can settle
down to work.

An amazing number of orchestra leaders have
come out of the studio bands employed by the
radio networks. Not so many years ago Benny Goodman was flitting from studio to studio over at CBS,
sitting in bands along with Tommy Dorsey, Jimmy
Dorsey, Bunny Berigan and a host of others. Since
that time, the CBS studio band has brought out
Will Bradley and Raymond Scott. These men didn't

bring orchestras to New York. But because they stood out as brilliant instrumentalists or composers, bookers selected them to lead bands. Will Bradley once sat in with Goodman's orchestra as a substitute for trombonist Vernon Brown, who was sick. None of the men, least of all Will himself, had any premonition of his sudden rise to fame as a leader. Bradley was really a fine boy and everybody was fond of him. But leading a band seemed the farthest thing from his mind. And it probably was! But it just happened that one of the important booking agencies wanted a certain type of band to pit against competitors. Nothing already on the market could meet their demands. So they decided to manufacture an orchestra overnight. They had heard Bradley play trombone at CBS, liked his musicianship, his face and his personality. So the William Morris Agency decided to sink a fortune in the man of their choice. They fished Will out of the CBS studio band and in less than a year Will Bradley's orchestra, a ranking favorite with dance fans, had played a sensational three-week holdover engagement at New York's Paramount Theater and was ready to go into the staid Biltmore Hotel. In other words, radio is a school for bandleaders.

Getting a job as a musician at CBS, NBC, ABC or Mutual headquarters in New York is difficult because it's the dream of most young men in the field. Radio really offers steady employment to musicians. Some of the men stay in house bands for years. There are no late dance-hall hours, no days on buses or sleepless nights on trains. The minimum pay, established by the New York Union, is $151.80 a week. But most of the staff players average from $175 to $300. That's because they supplement their regular studio salaries by playing on sponsored programs. A sponsored show requiring long hours of practice may pay as high as $85 for the complete day's work, which includes two broadcasts, one late at night for the West Coast.

Breaking into radio can be accomplished in two ways. A high recommendation from a musician already employed in a studio band will warrant giving you a try-out. Of course, you've got to wait for an opening on your particular instrument; and there's an old saying, "Few die, and none resign." The only other entrée comes through an audition with the special union contractor who hires men when vacancies occur. These contractors are important middlemen between the networks and the union. With offices in the network buildings, they are excellently placed as union watchdogs. Obtaining an audition is not an impossibility, even for unknowns. Louis N. Shoobe, contractor at CBS, has hired hundreds of musicians in his many years of faithful service to radio and to the union. His high standards and good musical taste have helped fill CBS bands and symphonies with individuals possessing qualities of leadership in their own right.

Don't bring an orchestra to these auditions. Only sponsors hire orchestras—famous orchestras. Networks also broadcast the music of celebrated bands, provided they play in hotels and night clubs that pay for the line charges. But the bands employed steadily for studio work consist of fine individual musicians. The aggregation is never hired as a lump or fired en masse.

I think we've gone as far in the business of jobs as words can take us. Most of the rules have been set before you. The consuming power of musical America is enormous. There's a place for your band, if it's a good band. Don't worry about the breaks. Breaks aren't luck so much as they are the result of outstanding ability coupled with persistent effort. Things will break when there's something on the ball.

CHAPTER VII

A DAY WITH AN ORCHESTRA
LEADER

9 A.M. Bandleader is awakened by telephone message from business manager, who has instructions never to call before ten. Latter says he's sorry but wants to know if boss is willing to appear at charity affair the following afternoon. Bandleader says playing for nothing is all right with him if it's all right with the union. Tries to go back to sleep, but mind is abuzz with ideas for his chorus on "Rosetta." Decides he may as well get up. While getting dressed, he plays a private recording submitted by a hopeful vocalist from his home town. The tenth such request to arrive in two weeks, the recording was accompanied by a letter which read, "I'm sure you can do something for Katinka Schultz; remember her?" Makes a mental note to have publicity man compose diplomatic letter to Katinka Schultz—something about her voice being beautiful but not suitable for hot orchestra requirements. Goes down to hotel Coffee Shoppe for breakfast. Orders from

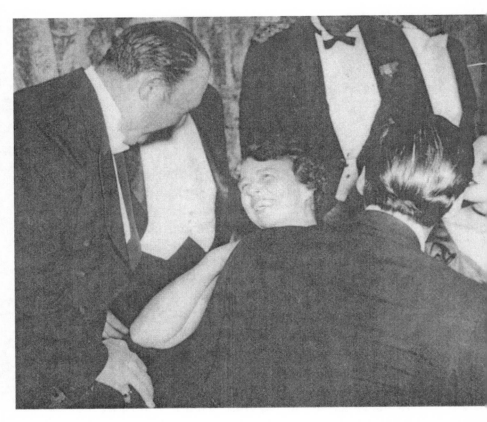

"My Day" fits into the bandleader's day. Paul Whiteman meets
Mrs. Roosevelt.

menu, and then signs it for waiter's nephew. Is besieged upon his exit from dining room by three high school students, who dart at him from cloakroom hiding place. One wants an audition on a ten-cent toy whistle, another just an autograph and the third a candid snapshot for his school paper. Maestro begs out of audition, but gives autograph and poses for picture. Shudders to think of what press agent will say to posing for a picture before he has even shaved his heavy beard. Goes back to room and wistfully swings a mashie niblick on the carpet. This bandleader owns four sets of sticks, belongs to five golf clubs scattered over the country and hasn't been able to sneak out to any of them in over a year. Phone rings. Publicity man wants to know if boss saw the break—a mention of his name—in Nick Kenny's radio column. Also says he's got a swell idea to land boss on first page of every paper in the country. Wants to have somebody in Oregon ship a cow by airplane as a present to bandleader, and then set it loose on Central Park "grazing pastures" as a big gag. Bandleader quickly quashes idea. Cow in airplane would get him in bad with humane societies. Cow in Central Park would mean row with police. Publicity man, disappointed, reminds him not to forget about the appointment later in the day with a feature writer from *Coronet*. Bandleader shaves.

10 A.M. Secretary from office comes over with twenty salary checks for boss to sign. Including office force, arrangers and musicians, rehearsal expenses, rents and transportation fees, the weekly outlay totals $4,500. Some of the checks he signs for musicians in the band come to around $125 for a week's work. On the other hand, one or two key men in the band get as high as $300 per week. Door buzzer interrupts painful signatures. It's the tailor to take his measurements for the new winter costume ordered for the band. Bandleader autographs tailor's tape measure and rushes out for next appointment.

11 A.M. Takes taxi to advertising agency representing his sponsor, for a conference on next week's broadcast. With a once-a-week show this meeting usually comes the day after the broadcast, which means that at least half an hour will be devoted to listening to records of preceding night's program, and discussing improvements. Then the subject turns to the following week's show: What musical selections will be played? Does it look like a well-balanced program? What will the specialty be? And so on. The meeting may include the advertising manager of the sponsoring concern, the account

Benny Goodman computes his income tax with the aid of Western Union telegraph blanks. It's all part of a day's—or year's—work in the life of a bandleader.

executive of the advertising agency, the production man who handles the show for the agency, the director of the broadcast—and if there's a dramatic script spot in it, an agency publicity man, the man who writes the commercial announcements, a copy writer who does the script introducing the musical numbers, and a handful of interested executives. The leader must know these men and try to give them what they want—without changing his style or doing anything out of character. The bandleader sometimes brings a weekly publicity clipping book to these meetings to keep the sponsor aware of the band's wide popularity.

NOON. Leader breaks away from agency pow wow for lunch at Lindy's with representative from a Midwestern state fair, interested in hiring band for a week's appearance. This conversation will take place in the presence of the bandleader's business manager, whose varied tasks may include booking jobs, arranging transportation, collecting the money on one-night stands, drawing up contracts between the leader and the men in the band, balancing the budget, auditing the books, paying taxes and handing out pink slips (dismissal notices). There are two kinds of managers. One discovers an obscure band, and by his hard work makes it famous. That kind of manager actually manages the leader. The other

Here's Larry Clinton, popular leader and composer of *Dipsy Doodle*, listening dreamily while his orchestra runs down a tricky arrangement at the Victor record studio.

type comes along after the orchestra leader is already a fairly big success. He is more of a routine-and-detail man, with the bandleader having the last word as to what jobs he'll play and what jobs he won't play. In this particular case, the bandleader gulps his coffee and lets the manager work out the details for the state fair job, which looks okay.

12:40 P.M. Meets three of his arrangers in a small NBC studio and begins by apologizing for having eaten lunch and making the arrangers wait. He has a list of numbers that have been picked for the next week's program. Some of them are repeats, but there are three new arrangements to be made. Bandleader gives each arranger an idea of the general form and the tempo he wants in finished product. The sponsor has suggested a medley of songs about roses to tie in with big flower shows being held at this season of the year all over the country. Bandleader considered the idea pretty trite, but has submitted without a murmur to sponsor's wishes. Now, with his arrangers, he chooses "Roses of Picardy," "Only a Rose," and "Rose of the Rio Grande" for the big presentation number. After the discussion is over, arrangers go home to piano while the leader hops into another taxi for his next commitment.

1:15 P.M. Still fifteen minutes behind schedule, leader shows up at the Decca recording studio

Here's a recording date with musicians carefully picked from various bands by Milt Gabler, standing in rear, who issues special "swing classic" records sponsored by his Commodore Music Shop, gathering place for New York swing fans. Bobby Hackett, trumpet, and Joe Marsala, clarinet, have their backs to the camera. George Wettling is at the drums, Jess Stacy on piano, Eddie Condon, guitar and Artie Shapiro, bass violin.

where his band is slated to cut four sides. Stops in upstairs first to pay courtesy call on executives of recording concern, listen to rival bands' waxings not yet on the market, and get a report on how his own discs are selling. The whole band is already going through its paces when the leader walks into the recording studio. Microphone balance has to be perfect—a job already attended to, after a lot of switching back and forth, by the record studio's permanent production man. After supervising rendition of each number, bandleader listens to playback and hunts for clarinet squeaks, sour notes, bad chords in improvised passages or any other noticeable flaw. Sometimes four or five tries are necessary before the leader says, "Wrap it up." By four o'clock the band has recorded four numbers—one of which, everybody hopes, may strike the public's fancy to the tune of 100,000 or more sales.

4:15 P.M. The leader dashes over to his booking agent's office where he has an appointment to go over charts for his next two-months tour. Some important orchestras entrust obtaining engagements for the band not to personal managers, who have enough to do, but to immense booking agencies with tentacles all over the country. There is a discussion of the distance between various towns, and the booker's traffic man is called in. On tour, the band must have a chance to sleep and eat as well as play. This conference is terribly important, because one error in booking may disrupt a whole schedule, may throw the band into confusion for a week. Once a famous conductor, having transported his mammoth orchestra to Europe for a long tour, suddenly remembered he was supposed to appear for a week's engagement in Florida. There was nothing to do but cart the whole company back to America. Then they returned to Europe right away. But somebody's oversight had caused a terrific loss of money and a lot of unnecessary seasickness.

5 P.M. The man of the hour sprints across the street to the radio studios for a short rehearsal. He's to appear in person on "Us Folks" to tell about his collection of Indian arrowheads. Finds prepared script has ten mistakes. Goes into conference with script writer. Decides to ad-lib. Sees a couple of musicians in studio band he used to play with. Sticks around for a little chat.

5:30 P.M. Steps in at 48th Street Music Store on the way to hotel to buy 200 Van Doren saxophone reeds. Finds that a shipment of saxophones has just arrived from France and so he looks them over. Returns to hotel room to dress for orchestra's dinner-hour session downstairs. The publicity man arrives with a reporter from *Coronet*, who gets a story on "Is Swing on the Way Out?" Manager calls up to say that *Variety* is coming out with a special anniversary issue and is soliciting an ad. Orchestra leader gives his approval for insertion of half-page "ad" wishing *Variety* good luck.

7 P.M. Plays and leads the band for two-hour session. Puts on floor show, introducing Argentine dancers and magician in addition to his own troupe. Sits with important people during short intermissions. Refuses six drinks, shakes hands with twenty-seven people, signs eighteen menus.

9:15 P.M. At radio station for guest appearance on air, which is broadcast from 9:30 to 10 P.M.

10:30 P.M. Back at his hotel job for steady grind. Prepares eight numbers for broadcast pickup from hotel at 11:30. Signs refreshment check for five swing critics who brought their girls down to hear the band. Listens between sets to song pluggers, talks to a columnist and meets his girl vocalist's mother, who's in town from Burlington, Iowa.

11:30 P.M. High tension for half an hour while band broadcasts dance music to the nation. Everybody has to be on his toes. One bad note might get a million laughs. Bandleader says "Hello, Everybody" on the air as if he hasn't a care in the world.

MIDNIGHT. Sits down for evening meal at table in corner. Waiters establish cordon to keep crowds

This nest of thrushes has chirped for millions. Find a girl who looks and sings like one of the above, and success is on your payroll. From left to right (top): Lena Horne, Berryl Davis; (bottom): Dinah Shore, Ginny Simms.

away and enable him to eat peacefully in "neutral zone." Band manager breaks through with announcement that one of the taut bull fiddle strings just snapped, catching the bass violin player on the chin and almost knocking him out. Leader interrupts meal and consoles musician as house doctor applies bandage.

2 A.M. Dance session is ended, but leader's day is not yet completed. An insurance agent has been waiting since one o'clock to obtain the leader's version of a payroll robbery in Erie, Pennsylvania. The leader had been proffered $2500 in cash as payment for a one-nighter, but refused to accept cash for fear of being robbed. The manager of the dance hall accordingly agreed to accompany the leader to a hotel where the money could be deposited and a check made out. As they were about to enter an automobile, they were accosted and robbed. Since the leader had refused to accept the money, the manager was holding it and had to stand the loss. He was insured, but the company wanted to check up on the story from the young leader's lips.

2:30 A.M. Crawls into bed. Dreams about music.

The day is over but the melodies linger on. No day in the life of a
bandleader is ever complete without at least one encounter with
song publishers. Here's a bevy of important tune salesmen offering
their wares to the late Hal Kemp.

The bandleader is a hero to millions of Americans. Here are Paul Whiteman and Benny Goodman in action, surrounded by both the "intellectual" and dancing species of jitterbug.

CHAPTER VIII

YOUR BEST FRIENDS—THE MUSIC FANS

PEOPLE in India have believed for centuries that flute-playing attracts mosquitoes. In America, experience proves that all instruments exert a magnetic power — on jitterbugs. But there's one big difference that needs to be pointed out. In India, as elsewhere, mosquitoes bite the instrumentalist. Over here, a lot of bandleaders bite the jitterbug— the hand that feeds them. And that bite is poisonous, not for the jitterbug, but for the orchestra leader who is doomed to failure without the swing fans' support. Maybe you're boss of the band, because you pay the men's salaries. But, like all executives, you're the servant of your own cash customers. That's something you can't learn too early in the game. Two paths lie open to the rookie orchestra director. He can take the high-hat road, keeping his distance from the "morons" far below him. That's the starting point for a quick finish. The alternative is to treat his followers as every businessman treats his clients—with courtesy, gratitude and a ceaseless desire to please.

Never before in history has any art possessed such a large consuming class as American music does today. The "patrons" of swing are mostly of high school and college age. Older people aren't patrons, because it's impossible to learn a foreign language like swing late in life. To the older generation, swing sounds like noise and discord. They insist it's not music, just the way any person of the Western world might insist that Chinese, spoken coherently by 400,000,000 people, is a gibberish. So, as a bandleader, your wagon is hitched to millions of devoted and faithful little jitterbugs, who'll plug for you as long as you play fair with them.

I had a talk recently with a sour bandleader who had just reached the top. "You know," he said with a hang-dog look in his eyes, "these swing fans really give me a pain in the neck. My life is one big traffic jam—the way they crowd around and hound me for autographs. On the next job I'm going to bring along a fourteen-foot pencil and leave my fourteen-piece band at home. Boy, am I looking forward to the day when I can tell some of those brats where to head in!"

A few years ago this "big shot" was playing horn in a honky-tonk jam band. Like most of the other hot-men of that pre-swing period, he longed for some recognition and appreciation of his improvised style of playing. But nobody gave him a tumble. In those days, even the great soloists had become reconciled to a life of "art for art's sake," a feeling of martyrdom and self pity being their only consolation. But suddenly something clicked, and swing caught on. Bunches of ogle-eared worshipers began haunting the space around bandstands. For the first time in his life our horn-blower friend heard his choruses cheered and applauded. Jitterbugs praised his songs and sang his praises. With these disciples hurrahing at his heels he landed a radio commercial, a record contract, movie shorts, a hotel job and all those things he'd always pined for. Translated into music to his ears, that meant anywhere from one to eight thousand dollars a week. And that's the fellow who was knocking the jitterbugs!

Swing music would still be floating in the bulrushes if the youth of America hadn't discovered it. Remove these devotees from the scene and you double unemployment among musicians in this country. They've increased our dance hall, concert and stage attendance by a third in the last few years. Thanks to these followers of hot music, scores of tumbled-down dance halls have been rejuvenated and turned into profitable ventures. Before the birth of the jitterbug, an orchestra could never dream of drawing large matinee crowds. Standees always existed at dances—but they were just wallflowers. Today, in addition to, say, 4,000 dancers, we get a thousand "intellectual" jitterbugs who come just to listen. The swing fan is probably the only entertainment-seeker in the world who isn't frightened away by the sign, "Standing Room Only." When he likes you, he organizes Benny Goodman, Vaughn Monroe, or Harry James fan clubs, always ready to rally to your side when you need him most. These fan clubs vote solidly behind you in the important popularity polls conducted by swing magazines like *Down Beat* and *Metronome*. No other commercial enterprise in the world can boast of customers who lavish their money on a product and then spend precious time and enthusiasm trying to put that product over on a national scale—just for the fun of it.

These are your customers—the people you'll have to get along with. They'll pull for you with all their might. Your job is to give them real music and treat them like the friends they are. It may mean signing autographs on match boxes, plaster casts, phonograph records, tuxedo shirts and snare-drum heads; it may mean answering a lot of funny questions, getting marooned in a turbulent ocean of

Paul Whiteman and young friends. Those eyes tell the story.

high-school students outside the stage door, or a thousand other petty inconveniences. But, that's a pretty small price to pay for being a hero. In fact, I think of it, not as a price, but in some small measure, as repayment for what the boys and girls of America have done for me.

And now it's up to you! You have chosen a profession rich in spiritual and material rewards. In the country you live in, nothing can retard or prevent your success except your own weaknesses and mistakes. That, I believe, is the strongest parting message I could leave with you. In no other great country could a man end a book with the words, "It's up to you." They would sound empty and ridiculous in lands across the ocean where individual enterprise has been blotted out and where the happiness and destinies of individuals are "up to the government"—and nobody else. I just want you to think, as you improvise a chorus—how much swing depends for its freedom on the principles of American democracy. Swing music wasn't mentioned in the Bill of Rights, and yet it is implied just as surely as freedom of the press. Freedom of the press gives journalists the right to editorialize on the news. What is a swing chorus? It is a musician editorializing on somebody else's melody. America has been a jam session ever since its beginning. The town meeting halls were places where everybody came to blow his own horn, and Congress is a forum where everybody comes to grind his own axe.

Swing, believe it or not, isn't taught in saloons and dance halls—but in the textbooks of our country's schools. We have told our children, "The best books haven't been written, the highest skyscrapers are still unbuilt, the smoothest roads haven't been laid out, and the biggest fish are still in the ocean." Give a boy with that education an airplane and he flies the Atlantic. Give him a set of tools and he perfects the automobile and produces it on a mass scale. Give him steel and concrete and he rears a skyscraper. Give him a musical instrument, and what happens? Is he content to play last century's music? Does he bow before a piece of manuscript and worship it as holy because its author is dead? Not on your tintype! Out of his saxophone will come a screech of rebellious freedom. It's his privilege, his pleasure and his art to make "Sweet Sue" sound like "Avalon" on Tuesday nights and like nothing ever heard before on Thursdays. His only obligation is to respect the laws of harmony and submit to the admonitions of good taste.

Improvisation is the earmark of musical freedom in America, just as it has always been the outward expression of history's only other completely un-handcuffed people—the Hungarian gypsies. Roaming around the melody is inevitable in a land where all the musical bars are down. What the layman must do is to realize that if he designs skyscrapers, takes a crack against the government, or sits on top of flagpoles—he is swinging Democracy in his own way. And no matter how battered an instrument you play now, the same Democracy that lets you "swing it" will also, in the long run, recognize your talent and reward tenacity and hard work with success. It has happened here a thousand times. And in the future there will have to be a thousand more men to fill the gaps left by the gradual disappearance of today's leaders. Here's a wish from the heart that you'll be among them!

CHAPTER IX

HOW TO BE A BANDLEADER

YOU are now about to attend a seminar course in the science of bandleading with "lectures" by ten outstanding professors—this country's ranking purveyors of dance music.

The authors have invited ten of our favorite maestros, whose music ranges from rhumba to re-and bebop, to present their own opinions on the most important factors making for band leadership. Read them all, find the common thread running through this remarkable orchestration of advice, and you can benefit from the bitter and sweet experiences of those who have already trodden the path on which you are just setting out.

By COUNT BASIE

We have all been brought up in the belief that Rome wasn't built in a day. In other words, everything worthwhile is worth working and waiting for.

But I'll go a step further and say that band leading is a life-time job. Almost no age is too early to start getting that firm foundation upon which one's later career must stand. I recommend particularly the six-year mark for the initial take-off so as to give the future baton waver time enough for a thorough legitimate musical background, which will eventually be well mixed with a good jazz feeling. A musician in this field should be endowed with an understanding of all forms of music, from classical to bebop.

Once you have mastered the art and science of music, the most important qualification is an individuality so unique that it is instantly recognizable. For example, Guy Lombardo, Duke Ellington, Benny Goodman, Tommy Dorsey and Sammy Kaye have this quality. Even if you're not a top instrumentalist, you can still be successful with a strictly personal style that clicks. Once this gets the public's stamp of approval, the rest is comparatively easy. Wherever possible, I feel the audience should be educated to a good leader's style rather than the leader catering down to the public's taste. However, this can't always be accomplished and the leader must, therefore, make some compromises. Any musical pioneering that a bandleader feels he must do can be sandwiched in between those numbers the public wants and demands.

Although you've got to have an individual style,

that doesn't mean that you shouldn't absorb some of the attractive qualities of early bands you may have played with. For instance, the influence of Benny Moten, with whom I was associated while I was still "growing up" musically, has never been lost in my present orchestra. Moten was a great exponent of Kansas City jazz. And it was this style that stayed with me as a bandleader and was the inspiration of our own highly-orchestrated style.

Showmanship is important, but must not be forced and should be suitable to the leader's personality. Although an attractive appearance is an asset, I'm sure you and I can both recall many topnotchers who wouldn't win any ribbons in beauty contests.

It is essential for a musical maestro to have an eagle eye for talent. You must be ready to lose many of your great stars and then be able to replace them with equally good ones.

As for getting the breaks, I feel that the music game has reached a point where the making of a hit record is one of the few guarantees of success. And a hit record is likely to be due to nothing more than a very lucky break.

Being a good business man is unnecessary. It's simple to hire good managers, agents, lawyers and publicity men. But it is good business to place complete trust in the people you choose and let them work unhampered.

How to Be a Bandleader

By Xavier Cugat

There are many bands and every type of leader imaginable, so if you want to join our ranks you must first decide upon your preference. If your choice is a quickly thrown together group of men—a fly-by-night combo where all that is required of the leader is that he stand up and wave a stick and show all his pearly molars to the non-discriminating patrons—this book is not for you. On the other hand, you may feel as I do that bandleading is a profession; a profession that requires a basic talent, a great degree of technical knowledge, an understanding and love for the work to begin with, and, as time goes on, something which demands growth, progress and contribution to that profession.

A bandleader must have something different to offer the public, be it a style which is inimitably his own, a new interpretation or approach, or a musical idea that he attempts to convey to his followers.

In 1930 I organized a six-piece orchestra of Cuban friends and played native rhumbas. Today the rhumba is loved and danced by millions of North and South Americans. But this was not the case back in the thirties. Then it was a dance for only the exotic, Spanish-type professional dance teams whose intricate and difficult steps made it natural for spectators to be discouraged from attempting it. To me, the rhumba was a dance which, if simplified, could be made pleasurable to everyone. I adopted the exciting rhythm of the rhumba as my "musical mission." I had been thoroughly trained in music and had performed many years as a concert violin soloist. Having been born in Barcelona and lived for many years in Havana, I was very familiar with the native music that has since become my specialty. Geography had equipped me well for the job I undertook. It is very important that you get the breaks at the start of your career. But it is even more important that you be well-prepared so that you can take advantage of these breaks when they do come.

Work hard at bandleading, for it is gratifying work, indeed. Take what is in your heart, apply to the knowledge in your mind, add the skill in your hands, and there you have the best formula for how to become a bandleader.

By Duke Ellington

The authors have allotted me several hundred words in which to capsule my prescription for musical glory. My advice can be distilled down to two words, that old Boy Scout motto: BE PREPARED.

By being prepared I do not mean just keeping

your trumpet valves well-oiled, your baton waxed, your tuxedo tie on straight, or your saxophones shined. For the bandleader, preparedness means a lot more than that. It means a readiness to say "yes" to every opportunity. It means having the hardihood to regard every opportunity as an obligation—an obligation to yourself, to the advancement of music, and to every man in your band. The acceptance of challenge is the only road leading out of the honky-tonk into Carnegie Hall.

Many years ago when our band, though already rocking, was still in its cradle, one of the biggest impresarios in the business offered us a week at the Palace Theatre in New York. In those days, the Palace was the garden spot of the vaudeville circuit, the best showcase in the country for budding bands. The invitation fell like a ripe plum right into our laps, a fact that was all the more remarkable since some of the top outfits in the bigtime had been trying unsuccessfully for years to nab a Palace engagement.

The day the offer came almost turned out to be doomsday for the fledgling Ellington aggregation, however. Yours truly still hadn't learned the secret of facing up to an obligation. "Duke," the theatre manager had warned, "if you take this engagement, you'll have to be your own master-of-ceremonies.

You'll have to announce the numbers and introduce the talent."

That was the rub. The mere thought of facing the audience instead of the music scared me half to death. I was a piano player fresh up from Washington, D. C., not a class valedictorian. One might as well have asked Demosthenes, the Greek orator, to perform a hot chorus on a lute.

Terror that my mind might go blank almost sidetracked fourteen musicians that day. It would have been easy to find an excuse for turning down the job. But it suddenly dawned on me that a bandleader must improvise many things besides hot choruses and something inside me forced me to say "yes."

A few seconds after the curtain came down on our first performance, the Palace manager rushed backstage. "Congratulations, Duke," he beamed. "You've developed a really fresh style as an emcee." It was fresher than he realized—as fresh as a morning hayseed.

Luck is everything, but it means nothing unless you're ready musically and morally to exploit it. Preparedness simply lies in ambush waiting for a chance to woo Lady Luck when she walks by. And she will—at least, once in a lifetime.

My own conception of luck can be defined as follows: being in the right place at the right time doing the right things before the right people. Luck, in all its pure partiality, shone dazzlingly on us one day two decades ago for one of the most crucial auditions of the band's career.

It was a try-out for the Cotton Club, whence our CBS broadcasts later won us nationwide attention. The audition had attracted several of the finest outfits in the country. One after another, they ploughed through their best arrangements, said their prayers, and packed up. It was an all-day joust for one of Gotham's juciest jobs, and the competition was so keen that a toss-up could have decided the winner. But there was only one trouble with all the bands that huffed and puffed the day away at the Cotton Club: they were doing the right things at the right place all right. But they weren't doing them before the right people: something had detained Irving Mills, the kingpin of the whole audition, and he didn't show up until late in the afternoon. He hadn't heard one note that came out of the vying orchestras. Ours was the only group he heard—because we arrived late—right along with Mr. Mills. We landed the Cotton Club dream-job because we were in the right place at the right (for us, anyway) time, doing the right things before the right person. Every ingredient of luck had conspired in our favor. And we were ready with the righteous music the moment the gods smiled our way.

As for our style of playing, its chief characteristics, maintained since 1923, have been: a spirit of organization and unity that is reflected in the comparative stability of our personnel; a continuity in the orchestra's sound and timbre which we owe to the similarity between Billy Strayhorn's and my scoring techniques; a happy distribution of solos among a brilliant array of improvisers; arrangements written especially as a framework to accentuate the peculiar talents of soloists like Johnny Hodges, Lawrence Brown, Ray Nance and all the others; and, finally, a strict avoidance of any kind of imitation or borrowing from the styles and mannerisms of other bands— and the toughest man not to imitate when we came to New York 24 years ago was the illustrious co-author of this book—good old "Pops" Whiteman, himself.

By Benny Goodman

Fourteen years in front of a band have convinced me that the greatest feat of magic consists not in becoming a bandleader—but in remaining one. There are hundreds of wide highways leading to the top, with well-wishers to help and cheer you along the climb. But once the heights are scaled, that's when you might find the perch too perilous for comfort. The well-wishers and glad-handers often drift away and even begin shooting popguns at you from their warm editorial caves.

The top you're aiming at resembles a slippery cake of ice. Standing still for a moment results in a case of cold feet. Sit down even for a moment and the competition may freeze you out. Bask for an aimless hour in the sunshine of your glory—and that ice paradise melts right out from under you .

The trick, as I say, lies in keeping your balance. Only one person can make you lose it. That's yourself. For just when you're entrenched on the pinnacle, the boys who once hailed you as "the greatest," "the hottest," and "the gone-est" will suddenly cast around for new loves to champion. And they won't let you fall lightly. The switching of their allegiance will be heralded by appropriate blowing of trumpets. You may suddenly find yourself denounced in some swing magazines as "the worst," "the corniest," and "the backwardest." If at that moment you don't have faith in yourself, if your music didn't come from the heart in the first place and can be altered simply because the critics changed their minds— then you're on the way to the land of bartered souls and sold-out musicians.

I speak from experience: a couple of years ago a coterie of swing critics, who are unable to play jazz, began condemning everyone who could except a tiny group of 52nd Street instrumentalists who specialized in bebop. The playing of all their former idols was carefully scrutinized. If their performances did not bristle with bebop ideas, these benighted instrumentalists were unceremoniously swept off the musical map. My clarinet was placed under quarantine. I was written off as "unprogressive" and the dreaded epithet of "mouldy fig" was flung at me by two or three outraged editorialists.

If at that moment I had believed in the critics more than in what music meant for me, I might as well have packed my clarinet in mothballs for life. For me to have gone over completely to bebop would have been a betrayal of something much more precious than the opinions of the magazine critics. Outside of four or five instrumentalists who bop naturally—and that includes the late Charlie Christian whom I was proud to have in my band before the word bebop was invented—the field is strewn with imitators. The lilting sound of the critics' praise is not enough to make me adopt something I never felt. Some bebop phrases and harmonic ideas have sunk deep into modern swing playing. They will find their way into our arrangements of their own accord. Fine musicians whose style falls into the bebop classification will also be welcomed in our aggregation. But I will continue to play as I feel.

My advice, then, pertains solely to staying on top: the style that put you there must have come from the heart because it incubated in the sincerity of your adolescence. Improve and advance, yes! But changing your style every time the critics bleat, letting the sidelines call the tune—that's the real commercialism, the *cheap* commercialism which these very critics claim to hate with all their heart. So—stick to your guns, your trumpets and clarinets, and play what rings true for you.

By Stan Kenton

Seven and a half years ago I would have found it mighty hard to tell anyone the requirements of being a successful bandleader. At that time I wished someone would tell me. I had just given birth to the idea of forming my own band and I had only two things to work with: an abundance of physical strength and a head-full of musical ideas. I was honest with myself. The type of band I wanted wouldn't be an easy one to sell. But I was going to prove something—or else.

There are lots of bands starting every day—some good, and some not so good. Swing bands and mickey-mouse. My aim was what was then called a "swing" band. The first financial hump was made easier by the fact that I was an arranger and didn't have to pay myself. Fortunately, too, I obtained men for the band who believed in my ideas and were willing to string along on unsensational salaries. Consequently, the band was formed without the usual borrowed money.

The first couple of years is the acid test—the years to hold fast to your ideals against every discouragement. I was criticized unmercifully for the music I was playing, but it reflected my feeling that something new was needed in the business. Everything was stagnant. You see, some bandleaders get a kick out of entertaining people with the tried-and-true music. There's no satisfaction in that for me. My greatest joy comes from creating something new. If that something new is accepted and appreciated, it provides the gratifying incentive which makes the whole music business worthwhile.

In my opinion, the prime requisite for a successful bandleader is that he be a musician—with a greater love of music than for the Almighty Dollar. It will take sacrifices for him to establish his unique ideas with the public. If and when his ideas are accepted, financial success will follow.

Today, more than ever, a bandleader must possess executive ability and a good booking sense. Living with his product, and with his pulse on the trend of public preferences, he is in a much better position to analyze booking needs than is the personal manager sitting in some far-off office.

A leader must also have an understanding of psychology, both for people individually and as an audience. Especially in dealing with musicians, whose talent is almost synonymous with temperament, only a high regard and understanding of their opinions can bring out the best performances.

The music business today is growing rapidly. The stature of jazz, too, is developing constantly. It is my endeavor to be an integral part in the history and advancement of jazz.

By Vaughn Monroe

The obvious answer to the question "How To Be A Bandleader" is that the aspiring maestro should first have a thorough knowledge of music—including the mastery of several instruments and, if possible, some vocal training. But good all-round musicianship is by no means the only qualification necessary to be a bandleader today.

Speaking from personal experience, I've found that an orchestra leader has to be a business man, psychologist, host, talent scout and showman—all rolled into one.

Running a band is a 24-hour-a-day job. A band-leader needs the heart of a hobo and more stamina than a gold rush pioneer. The boys and I are in a constant grind of one-nighters and theatre dates, in addition to making records for RCA-Victor, our weekly air stint for Camels and an occasional movie. Last year we played a hundred one-nighters, a two-month engagement at New York's Hotel Commodore, about 15 weeks of theatre dates and several one-week engagements at nightclubs; plus many personal appearances for benefits, on record programs and at record dealers.

No matter how good a musician you are, you still need Spartan strength to follow a steady schedule like that, which is why I consider good health a major requisite for anyone who wants to be a band-leader. I'm a sports enthusiast myself—tennis, golf, swimming, and horseback riding—and I've found that there's nothing better than outdoor exercise to develop coordination and general poise on a bandstand.

Another important qualification, not usually associated with the bandleading field, is a keen business sense. A name band is no plaything. It's big business, involving complicated contracts, elaborate bookkeeping, and a sizable staff of employees.

A good business course, with emphasis on

mathematics and bookkeeping, often spells the difference between success and failure for the beginning bandleader.

Perhaps the most important factor of all in determining final success, is your own personality. You should like people—and I mean *really* like them! Audiences can sense a phoney a mile away, and in the last analysis, no matter how good a musician you are, it's the audience's reaction to you that counts. A good part of the success I've obtained as a bandleader is because I've liked people.

You've got to get out on the road and meet your public to find out the kind of music they like. Trends in dance tempos are like women's skirts. They change overnight. And if a band stays in one spot too long it soon becomes as dated as last year's hemline. A bandleader is a front man and the ability to mingle with all types of people, easily and tactfully, is a tremendous asset in this business.

So, if you want to be a bandleader, here's how it stands: 1) You'll need a thorough background in the technical phases of music. (This will probably involve working as a sideman. I place a high value on my experience as a side trumpet man before forming my own unit.) 2) Good health. Establish and maintain the habit of keeping fit physically. 3) A keen business sense. 4) Be a good public relations man. 5) Pray for the "breaks."

By Guy Lombardo

A bandleader nowadays must be able to do more than just read music and wave a baton.

Naturally, he must know "music." A person who hasn't devoted a considerable portion of his youth to the study of music can never hope to be a success as a bandleader. He must have a thorough background in the classics and must know and understand all types of music, from the symphonies through bebop. There have been exceptions, but the vast majority of successful maestros are more than a little conversant with all kinds of music.

Furthermore, as new forms come into being, the bandleader, no matter how well established, must study them thoroughly. I consider it as much a part of my business to keep up with what Stan Kenton and Dizzy Gillespie are doing, as with what is being done by Benny Goodman, Freddie Martin, Kay Kyser, Vaughn Monroe and others.

No youngster can ever hope to crash into the big time immediately as an orchestra leader. For every one who achieves some measure of success, there are thousands who, try as they may, never get a foot through the front door.

If a youngster aspires to make his career in music he must, of course, be ready to take the knocks with the boosts, the good with the bad. He cannot, especially in these days, expect a bed of roses ahead of him.

If his goal is to lead an orchestra, he must first prove to himself that he is basically capable of achieving that goal. The wisest way to do this is to organize a commercial band in his own community. In doing so he will come across not only the problems of what to put into the band musically speaking, but against the hard business aspects as well. He will soon learn there is a law of supply and demand, and that because of the oversupply, only those orchestras that have the most to offer the public can survive and prosper.

In this early stage of leading a band, he will find he has to come up with a style that is different and pleasing to the public. The public either makes or breaks bands. The aspiring bandleader will soon learn that the quickest way to incur the public's displeasure is to ignore its requests for songs. He will learn that 80% of his success will depend on his ability to play the songs the public wants to hear. The remaining 20% will depend on his style, personality, the breaks and various other factors.

My own experiences have taught me that if the song being played is one the public wants to hear played, the people will dance to it and listen appreciatively. As soon as I see that no one is getting up to dance or that there is a buzz of conversation around the room, I know they aren't listening and aren't even interested in what's being played. This, of course, is my cue to take the song out of my books.

How many thousands of orchestra leaders-to-be have met with failure because they have insisted on trying to force songs down the public's throat when the public just will not be forced!

The orchestra business is like any other business in the world in that the bandleader must be a business man. No matter how big the crowds he draws, no matter how many records he sells, he must always keep aware of the fact that he has bills to meet and that his employers—the hotel owners, radio sponsors and the like—also have expenses to meet because of the band.

A bandleader's personality and appearance count for much. A ready smile, a firm handshake, signing autographs without displaying annoyance—all of these are definitely important. A bandleader or a band is nothing without a public. The public is, in the final analysis, the employer. The public has a right to be treated with respect and courtesy.

Appearance? Well, I, for one, always insist that my musicians be well-groomed, clean shaven and gentlemanly. It is not good business or good public relations to have musicians on your staff who sass the customers, who chew gum on the bandstand, or who present an unkempt appearance. Appearance does count—especially in these days when television looms large as a coming factor in music.

Behind the success story of every name bandleader you can find a long period of hard work, the ability to spot and make breaks.

Opportunity doesn't knock often. When it knocks, the bandleader must recognize that knock and be ready to answer.

CPSIA information can be obtained at www.ICGtesting.com
Printed in the USA
LVOW08s1815300516

490425LV00001B/29/P